PRAISE RELEASES FAITH

Transforming POWER For Your Life

Terry Law

VICTORY HOUSE PUBLISHERS
Tulsa, Oklahoma

PRAISE RELEASES FAITH
ISBN 0-932081-15-0
Copyright © 1987 by Terry Law
Terry Law Ministries
P.O. Box 92
Tulsa, Oklahoma 74101

Published by Victory House, Inc.
P.O. Box 700238
Tulsa, Oklahoma 74170

Contents

Dedicated to my wife, Shirley

I praise God for giving me a most precious gift in you.
You are His expression of love to me.
I am blessed beyond words.

1

Thought Attack

The Power of Praise and Worship

My life and ministry have been revolutionized by the praise and worship message. Some time ago I encountered a tragedy in my life, and I was able to make it through only when I learned the power of praise and worship. Shortly after that experience the Lord spoke to me and commissioned me to take His message of praise and worship to the church. He told me, *"If you will lead people into My presence through praise and worship, I will heal the sick, save the lost, and deliver the oppressed."*

I knew that this would involve a change in my ministry. Previously, my primary thrust had been in missionary evangelism overseas, but as the Lord spoke, I began planning to take the praise and worship message to people everywhere. I didn't realize what tremendous power would be released in my ministry as I followed the Lord's directing. It soon became obvious, however, as remarkable things began to happen.

For example, I remember one night in Canada when we were ministering to a congregation of 400. We witnessed a tremendous outpouring of the Holy Spirit. Many confessed to salvation and there were several physical healings. When the service was over, the pastor invited me to go into a Sunday school room. When I walked into the room, I looked into the eyes of a woman whose appearance brought a shudder to my being. Her eyes were half shut. They looked as if they were hooded. There was a dull, lifeless expression on her face.

Some of her friends had brought her to the meeting for deliverance. They explained that she had been in a mental institution for a year and a half. She had spent a good part of her hospitalization in a straight jacket. It became obvious to me that evil spirits oppressed her. At times, demonic entitities made her entirely unmanageable. When her friends brought her to the service that night, for instance, she became physically sick in the parking lot. The demons did not want her to attend our service.

The pastor looked at me and asked, "Is there anything you can do?" Knowing I was confronting the power of Satan's strongholds, I looked at the woman and began to speak to the evil spirits that bound her, "Release your hold on this woman. I command you, in the name of Jesus Christ to come out of her!"

I remembered the story in Acts 16 where a certain young lady who was oppressed with a fortune-telling demon had followed Paul through the streets of Philippi. She continually cried aloud, disturbing his ministry. Paul turned toward her and said to the evil spirit who inhabited her body, "I command thee in the name of Jesus Christ to come out of her!" And the fortune-telling spirit came out that same hour.

On that Scriptural basis, I spoke to the spirits within the former mental patient—not to the woman: "Evil spirits, in the name of the Lord Jesus Christ, I command you to name yourselves." Various spirits began to identify themselves even though the woman was in an almost comatose state. One by one, as they named themselves, the spirits released their hold on her. The sixth spirit surprised me when it called itself

"Mind Control." When that spirit came out of her, the woman looked at me and began to smile. Then she said something that startled me: "Oh, I can remember." Her obvious rejoicing revealed that this mind-control spirit had held her memory and thought processes in bondage. She received complete deliverance that night.

When I left the room, she was still standing with her hands raised, tears rolling down her cheeks, dancing and singing all around the room. There was great joy in the hearts of the people who brought her to the meeting that night. I breathed a prayer of thanksgiving to the Lord.

Mind Control

I have never been able to get that particular experience of deliverance out of my mind, *because it convinced me that Satan is in the business of mind control. He wants people's minds.* The Apostle Paul was concerned about this when he said, "But I fear, lest by any means, as the serpent beguiled Eve through his subtilty, so your minds should be corrupted from the simplicity that is in Christ" (2 Cor. 11:3). Paul knew of Satan's incredible ability to lead Christians away from Jesus. He knew, also, that the evil one wants to reach inside our minds with his corrupt suggestions and make us do things we don't want to do.

The subtilty which beguiled Eve is still with us today. The devil, at the beginning, simply placed a question in Eve's mind. He said, "Hath God said?" He appealed to the human mind and put it in opposition to the spirit.

Adam and Eve had walked with God in fellowship in the Garden. In fact, the Bible indicates that God would come to them in the Garden in the cool of the evening and they would walk and talk together.

This is a beautiful representation of fellowship. It

shows spiritual harmony. God gave them instructions concerning the Garden—what they could and could not do. The only thing they could not do was partake of the fruit of the tree of the knowledge of good and evil. When the serpent beguiled Eve, he simply placed a question in her mind concerning God's command. He encouraged her to think independently of God. He appealed to the ability of the human mind to think creatively on its own, outside of God's influence and spiritual direction.

When Eve listened to the serpent and took the fruit and gave it to Adam, something happened within the personality of mankind. Satan put disharmony at the core of man's being. To this day, the human mind remains in opposition to the spirit. That is why Paul warns us against permitting our minds to be corrupted by the subtilty of the devil.

Satan and Your Mind

The devil manipulates the minds of God's people with surprising ease. Have you ever noticed, when you are sitting in a gospel service, how easy it is for your mind to wander? Sometimes, even during a time of prayer, when you are thinking about the things of God, all of a sudden an idea—a perverse idea—or an evil thought will come into your mind, seemingly out of nowhere. You are shocked by it. The moment the thought enters your conscious mind it fills you with guilt. You may say to yourself, "How can I be so wicked? How could I think such a terrible thought?" You didn't realize where the thought came from, and so you accepted personal guilt for it.

As soon as you accept that guilt, the thought becomes yours. Did it ever occur to you that your thought was triggered by someone other than yourself? Satan is "the accuser of the brethren." Have you ever wondered why you cannot remember the Scriptures as you would like to? Satan is responsible. Our minds are often left wide open to his attack. If we don't watch the thoughts that come through our minds, Satan will introduce his own ideas into our thinking processes.

Most of the time we are not aware when he does this, and the evil thoughts appear to be our own. An undisciplined thought life makes one vulnerable to the devil. Thinking involves a contest. Evil strongholds of the devil are actively arrayed against you for the purpose of clogging up your mental processes. There are spiritual beings whose job it is to keep you from occupying your mind with the Word of God. There are evil spiritual powers that make it their business to bring sickness and disease to you. They spend their time triggering thought processes in your mind to keep you away from God.

Spiritual Warfare

Paul says, "For we wrestle not against flesh and blood, but against principalities, against powers, against the rulers of the darkness of this world, against spiritual wickedness in high places" (Eph. 6:12). Our battle is not with people. We are battling against spiritual beings. Paul calls these entities "principalities." The Greek word for principalities is *"arche."* In the present context, that word means, "first among rulers." *Arche* has been incorporated into the English language as the root word for archbishop or archangel. Therefore, we are wrestling with ruling princes.

Paul also uses the term "powers." In Greek the word for powers is, *"exousia."* It speaks of areas of authority that these spiritual beings control.

The third of these adversaries is "rulers of the darkness of this world." There are spirit beings, called rulers, who have set themselves against you and me. We are in a spiritual wrestling match with the rulers of the darkness of this world.

The fourth, and final evil-spirit personality that

Paul lists is "spiritual wickedness in high places." In the original Greek language, that phrase would be better translated as "wicked spirituals in the heavenlies," (heavenly places). Our wrestling match, therefore, is against spirit beings of tremendous ability and power. They are called principalities, powers, rulers, and wicked spirituals. Paul also tells us *where* these forces dwell—in heavenly places.

This means that in the spiritual world a full-scale military campaign has been mounted against every believer. The battlefield is the thought life of the Christian. Make no mistake about it—spiritual war is real. Satan knows that if he can influence the thoughts of your mind, he can control you. In fact, your mind is the major area of your life that he must touch. If he can't get at you through your mind, then he really can't get you at all. That fact may surprise you but it is nonetheless true.

Obviously, many of us are attacked in our bodies as well. Yet, most diseases we encounter come to us, through our minds, in the form of psychosomatic disorders. In order for us to understand the full impact of Satan's attack on the thought life, it is necessary to see the Scriptural background for it.

What Does Scripture Say?

In Acts 8, Philip went down to Samaria and was experiencing a tremendous revival. Many people were saved, healed and delivered from the power of Satan. After they had been baptized in water, Philip called Peter and John to come and lay hands on them so that they might be filled with the Holy Spirit. There was a man named Simon in Samaria who was attracted by the power manifested by Peter and John when they laid hands on people to receive the gift of the Holy Spirit. He offered them money so that he might receive that same power. Peter rebuked Simon and admonished him, "Pray, that the *thought* of thine heart might be forgiven thee." Simon had been fooled by the devil.

The devil had the ability to trigger an idea—a thought—that brought Simon under the judgment of God. Peter was saying in effect, "Satan has put this thought in your heart. You have accepted it as your own and acted upon it; therefore, you are responsible for it." Then he commanded Simon to ask God to forgive him for the thought. This illustrates the truth that our minds are constantly under an attack from the devil.

How does Satan trigger thoughts in our minds? Have you ever noticed what the Bible says concerning the betrayal of Jesus? "...the devil having now put into the heart of Judas Iscariot, Simon's son, to betray him" (John 13:2). Satan dropped a thought into the heart of Judas, but Judas became responsible for that thought when he made it his own. He acted upon it. He did something about it. Judas obviously had the ability to choose whether he would betray Christ or not betray Him, but he listened to the thought that Satan had planted in his mind, and acted upon it.

The enemy's primary approach is to drop a thought into our minds. He wants us to accept it, to buy it. When we do that, he has achieved his purpose in our lives. The primary place of satanic attack is in your mind and thought life. That's why so many of us are unaware of the reality of Paul's words in Ephesians 6:12, "For we wrestle not against flesh and blood, but against principalities, against powers, against the rulers of the darkness of this world, against spiritual wickedness in high places."

Thought Attack

Let me tell you a story. In 1978 I traveled into the Soviet Union with one of my Living Sound music and evangelism teams. We were staying in a hotel in a certain city. Each night we ate supper in a restaurant where a rock and roll band played. One night God gave me a thought. "Tell your musicians to get ready for a concert."

I suggested that they go to the leader of the band and offer their services. He was delighted to have a group of Americans perform for them. Our team did a forty-five-minute concert of gospel songs. Then the evangelist for the team shared a five-minute message concerning God's love for them and encouraged them to accept Christ as their personal Savior. There were over one hundred people present.

The effect was startling; some people applauded, others were angry. The young woman who was the star of the cabaret show for the hotel came under conviction. Her name was Marju. She came to our musicians and wanted to know more. She gave her life to Jesus about 3:00 A.M. that morning.

Her life was transformed. The next night in her show she shared with the people how God had changed her life. She did this every day for a week. The hotel management became upset and called in the secret police. She was fired from her job. But that didn't affect Marju. She simply moved down the street to the Methodist church and began to share her testimony there. Young people came by the score from as far away as a hundred kilometers. Finally it became necessary for her to flee the country for her own safety and to go to Stockholm, Sweden.

I visited Marju in Stockholm shortly afterwards. She was experiencing a tremendous battle with oppressive thoughts from her past life. I was aware of their satanic origin and prayed with her for her deliverance. God set her free in a remarkable way.

After our prayer time together I went back to my hotel room in downtown Stockholm. I was staying in the Y.M.C.A. I didn't realize we were situated in the very center of Stockholm's red light district. There were several sex shops on the streets outside the hotel.

I went to sleep exhausted by the day's activities. I had been sleeping for a short time and then began to stir. I was only semi-conscious. I was aware of some terribly foul thoughts in my mind. They were worse than anything I had ever thought before. I felt convicted by what I was thinking but then the thoughts seemed to say inside of me, "You are wicked. *Your heart is inexpressibly sinful for you to think something like this. We have a hold on you. We are inside of you.*"

By this time I was wide awake and very much aware of the fact that I had a spiritual battle on my hands. I began to pray in the spirit and commanded those thoughts to leave me. They didn't want to go. Finally after an hour, I sensed the oppression lift off me and I was set free. I realized that I had experienced a direct thought attack from Satan.

These spirit beings are warring in your mind. Those thoughts that assail you, that try to make you sick, that try to destroy your marriage, that bind up your finances—those thoughts are coming from the devil. Very few Christians realize this fact. They are unconcerned about guarding their minds. Their minds are easily filled with useless television programs. They allow their minds to be filled with the trash being shown on soap operas and other programs, and consequently, they open themselves to a direct attack from Satan.

Paul said, "Wherein in time past ye walked according to the course of this world, according to the prince of the power of the air, the spirit that now worketh in the children of disobedience" (Eph. 2:2). This verse describes the fantastic ability of the devil to control people. The prince of the power of the air is now working inside people. He is actively controlling the children of disobedience, but he is also working within the lives of those who are trying to follow God. The power of his operation is indicated in the text by the word "worketh": "...the spirit that now worketh." *The devil is working against you and me—now.*

The Bible says, "But those things which proceed out of the mouth come forth from the heart; and they defile the man" (Matt. 15:18). Most of us have not understood the central focus of the next verse: "For out of the heart proceed evil thoughts." Murders are evil thoughts, adulteries are evil thoughts, fornications are evil thoughts, thefts are evil thoughts, etc. Evil thoughts result in evil acts.

Spirits Operate Through Thoughts

In all of my experience with demon spirits I have discovered that all of them want to control certain realms of human thought. Fear is a thought, suicide is a thought, murder is a thought, depression is a thought, alcholism is a thought. These thoughts come against you from the devil because he wants to create a stronghold in your life. He wants his kingdom to be established inside of you. He wants your effectiveness in the Kingdom of God to be destroyed. If he can't destroy it absolutely, he will at least rob it of most of its effect by getting you off base in some part of your life.

After Jesus had risen from the dead, He appeared to His disciples and said these words, "...Why are ye troubled? and why do thoughts arise in your hearts?" (See Luke 24:38). He knew why they were troubled. They were troubled because of the thoughts that arose in their hearts. Their fear was directly connected with their thoughts. Thousands of people today are gripped by that same kind of fear. Their hearts are troubled and they have never realized that the fear that created the troubling of their hearts came from the thoughts of Satan. We are responsible when we accept those thoughts. Many of us have lived for years in the torment that those thoughts have produced.

One of the most powerful verses regarding Satan's ability to influence our minds is given in the teaching of the Parable of the Sower: "When any one heareth the word of the kingdom, and understandeth it not, then cometh the wicked one, and catcheth away that which was sown in his heart" (Matt. 13:19). Let us examine that verse for a moment and try to see the power that Satan has to enable him to do something like that to you or me. He is not only present, but he **knows** what is going on in the mind of the listener. What kind of ability is required to do this?

Recently, I was invited to speak to a group of men in a conference outside of Honolulu, Hawaii. I was discussing with them Satan's power in this area. One minister spoke up and said, "We have always been taught that Satan cannot read our thoughts. Is this true?" My reply was simple. "Have you ever seen a sign advertising a mind reader. There are people who operate in the occult and do have the ability to read minds. They get that ability from familiar spirits."

Mind Reader

Our minds are exposed to Satan's view. He is aware when we do not understand the gospel. He knows if our minds are darkened, and he immediately fires thoughts that are contrary to the gospel presentation. But the above verse indicates that there is a satanic power as well; he has the power **to take the truth away.** He can snatch the Word of God right out of a man's mind. How does he do that?

Do you remember what Peter said to Ananias and Sapphira? "...why hath Satan filled thine heart to lie to the Holy Ghost...?" (Acts 5:3). That is a frightening question. Satan had filled the heart of

Ananias with a lie. Ananias had been a child of God—the enemy had snatched the Word of God out of his mind and had filled his mind with his lies. *It is obvious from this Scripture that Satan definitely has the ability to introduce his own ideas into our thinking processes.*

This is the key to understanding the devil's power against you and me. Clearly the center of spiritual warfare is in our minds. If Satan can keep Christians from meditating on God's Word, then he is successful. If he can cause our minds to be occupied with the trivia of the day, he has been successful. If he can trigger our minds to introduce his ideas—if he makes our minds wander during the proclamation of the gospel, then he has been successful.

That's why Peter encouraged us to "gird up the loins of our mind." He says, "Be sober, be vigilant; because your adversary the devil, as a roaring lion, walketh about, seeking whom he may devour" (1 Pet. 5:8). How does the enemy devour God's people? By controlling our thoughts. He is like a hunter stalking his prey. He lurks in the darkness. He studies you. He knows you better than you know yourself. He takes an idea, and faster than an arrow flies from a bow, that idea is triggered in your mind. You think the thought, you feel it is yours, you accept the guilt for the thought, and as soon as you do, he wins the battle.

Satan is called "the accuser of the brethren." Not only does he accuse us day and night before God in heaven, but he accuses us to **ourselves** daily in our own minds.

The Power of Guilt

The greatest power Satan will manifest in the heart of a believer is the power of guilt. He has manipulated believers for centuries with the power of guilt, and the memory of past sin. He literally haunts our minds with memories of things we have done. This is a part of his power to hold us and to control us. Only when we use the keys that enable us to break the hold guilt has on our minds, do we experience spiritual victory.

Many people think that when they become a Christian, when they confess Jesus as their Lord and Savior, that the battle is over. They feel cleansed inside. Their life is all fresh and new, yet their fight with the devil is not over. The moment that you declare Christ as your Savior, the war trumpet sounds. A new conflict begins immediately. When you were born again, you enlisted in the army. You can depend upon the fact that the power of evil will move against you as never before and that a battle will rage for the control of your thought life.

The great demand God puts upon the life of a new Christian is the need for a renewed mind. Romans 12:1, 2 says:

> **1 I beseech you therefore, brethren, by the mercies of God, that ye present your bodies a living sacrifice, holy, acceptable unto God, which is your reasonable service.**
> **2 And be not conformed to this world:** *but be ye transformed by the renewing of your mind,* **that ye may prove what is that good, and acceptable, and perfect, will of God** (italics mine).

Paul encourages us not to be conformed to the world. That means we are to avoid the world thoughts Satan attempts to put in our minds. Don't think those thoughts. Don't watch television programs that encourage "worldly thoughts." Don't listen to gossip. Don't look at pornographic magazines or videos. Don't experiment with drugs. Don't do anything that opens your mind to an attack from the enemy. "Be not conformed to this world: but be ye transformed by the renewing of your mind."

Spiritual Metamorphosis

In the original Greek, the word "transform" is *"metamorphose."* As you know, a metamorphosis takes place when a caterpillar turns into a butterfly. When a person is saved, his spirit is recreated. The born-again person becomes a new creature in Christ, but that doesn't mean that his mind has been renewed. This renewing process is a major part of the Christian warfare.

The renewing of the mind happens in several ways. We renew our minds by meditating on the Word. We renew our minds by praying in the Spirit. We renew our minds by entering into the power of praise and worship. When we decide we will have a renewed mind, Satan attacks. He is terrified of a believer who is committed to renewing his mind. He moves in with a terrific onslaught of evil suggestions. The last thing in the world Satan wants is a changed mind which produces a changed life.

Paul writes, "And be renewed in the spirit of your mind" (Eph. 4:23). Satan is pleased when he can hold onto the mind of a Christian. His fight to dominate us at that point becomes a furious all-out assault and the sad fact is that many believers have been serving the Lord for ten or twenty years and they are still under Satan's domination in their thought life. This is primarily because they are ignorant of the way the devil works. *Satan's dominion over you will last until you decide to fight against him.*

Our minds are like computers. The mind never stops operating. Feed it with thoughts of Jesus and it produces thoughts of Jesus, but when you feed the computer of the mind with thoughts of the world, you produce a worldly man. Satan is a master at programing our mental computers. That's how he exercises his control over us. Because he cannot touch our wills, he must find a way to influence our wills and he does that through our minds.

Master of Suggestion

Satan does not have the ability to control your thoughts; he is simply a master of suggestion. He will trigger a memory from the past. He will trigger something out of our subconscious and immediately a temptation comes to us. The enemy knows that our thought life so affects our wills that we are said to be the product of our thinking. That's why the Scriptures say, "As a man thinketh in his heart so is he." As long as you give Satan the opportunity to program your mind's computer, you will be under his control.

His strategies are varied. He is not necessarily interested in making you commit a terrible sin. Perhaps he has chosen, in your case, to render you ineffective in a different way. He is happy if you live in a moral life and do good things, as long as your life is essentially wasted otherwise. He really doesn't care if you have a church position or whether you are on the deacon board, as long as he can render you ineffective. There are thousands upon thousands of believers who attend church every Sunday, fit beautifully into society, have good families, and yet essentially do nothing in the Kingdom of God. There is no burden on their hearts to reach the world, to make an impact on their communities for the Kingdom of God. The enemy has put them to sleep. That is just one of Satan's strategies.

If Satan has access to our minds, how does he exercise control over them? Can he literally control our thinking? Is he allowed to interfere with our choice of thoughts? Can he violate our free will by making us think what he wants us to think? No, he cannot do these things.

God Himself does not violate our privilege of free choice. **Satan has the ability to suggest evil** *thoughts to us, but we are not responsible for those suggestions until we make them our own.* We make a choice in that process. Even faith is based on our ability to choose. Faith is a response to divine revelation. If God does not allow Himself to violate our free will, He will not allow the devil to do it either. If God would give such permission to the devil, we would no longer be responsible for what we do. We would simply be able to shrug our shoulders and, with a smile like that of a well-known comedian, simply say, "The devil made me do it!"

When Are You Responsible?

Satan wants us to be responsible for our actions. He wants us to be judged for wickedness—the wickedness he inspired. Therefore, he devises creative means for reaching through our minds to influence our wills. Once you make the all-important decision to accept the thought as your own, then he knows he's been successful.

Let us summarize the enemy's ability to influence our thought life:

1. He has access to our minds.
2. He is able to trigger thoughts and imaginations, motives, ambitions, longings.
3. Because he knows where we are weak, he is able to probe and manipulate those vulnerable areas.

Remember, he knows you better than you know yourself. We have forgotten most of the things we have done over the years. Satan has not. It is all tucked away in our memory system somewhere. He is an expert at probing that memory system and triggering the kinds of ideas and guilts that put us under his control. He does it all simply by making a suggestion, but because he is such an expert, his suggestions take on an awesome power.

We live by suggestion. A creative idea is a suggestion. The great inventions of the world have been suggestions. Revelation from God is a suggestion. We are led by the Spirit of God within us through suggestion.

Murder Exposed

Let me illustrate this truth with an anecdote. In January, 1985, my associate Don Moen and myself were conducting a Praise and Healing Crusade on the East Coast. At the end of the Sunday night service (there were about 1200 people in the meeting), I gave a call for people to make a commitment to Christ. I have learned to be sensitive to God's thoughts during these altar calls. On this particular night I received a very powerful impression from the Holy Spirit. It was so strong I literally heard myself speaking the words before I realized what I was saying. I said, ***"There is a man in this meeting tonight who is planning to kill his wife.*** You have purchased the gun and you are waiting for the moment. The Holy Spirit has instructed me concerning this to bring you under conviction. God wants you to know that He is aware of your plan. I am going to wait at the altar when this meeting is over because I want to point you to Jesus Christ as your personal Savior."

Believe me, I had everyone's attention. An audible gasp escaped from the crowd. All the ladies were looking at their husbands. When the meeting was over, I waited at the altar but no one approached me. I went home that night perplexed.

The next day several people called the pastor's office. They thought it was improper for an evangelist to terrify the audience that way. The pastor encouraged them to wait and see what God would do.

This particular crusade went on for three days. On Monday night we experienced a tremendous manifestation of healing power. Several folks testified to the fact that they had witnessed a "cloud of glory" over the altar and chancel area. God began to heal the sick who were scattered throughout the audience. I noticed a man on my left move out to the aisle and walk rapidly to the front. He knelt down and began to pray. Immediately a church counselor joined him and they prayed together. After twenty minutes had passed, the counselor walked up to me and whispered, "The man who was planning to kill his wife, has just committed his life to Christ."

I was overjoyed. I returned home to Tulsa eager to share the story with others. I told the story on my daily radio program that aired in seventeen different markets across the United States and Canada. I was careful to hide the identity and location of the man.

Three weeks later, I received a letter from a man in Phoenix, Arizona. He told me a strange story. He had been driving on a freeway in Phoenix. He had purchased a gun and was planning to kill his wife. He decided to listen to the radio and began to tune in to various stations on the dial. He happened to tune in to my program just as I began to tell the story I have just related to you. **He said it was as if God began to speak to him through the radio.** He pulled his car over to the shoulder. A wave of Holy-Spirit conviction came over him and he began to repent. He raised his hands to God and began to weep. He became a child of God that day and immediately changed his behavior toward his wife. Their marriage was restored and their personal lives transformed.

God's Thoughts and Suggestions

This is a dramatic illustration of the power of God's thoughts. There is no way, in the natural, that I could have known about that man. I received what the Bible calls a "word of knowledge" (1 Cor. 12:8). *It was just one of God's suggestions.* I believe those suggestions are coming to us all the time. Most of us are just not sensitive enough to hear what God is saying.

In other words, we are suggestive beings. Therefore, the devil is committed to controlling our minds through satanic suggestion. How fiendishly clever he is. He waits until the right time and the right moment. He waits until our guard is down. He understands where we are weak better than we do. Suddenly the thought is in our mind. The opportunity to respond to the thought is in front of us. We remember the guilt associated with having responded to that thought before. He suggests you've done it before, you might as well do it again. How easy it is at that point to accept the suggestion—to respond by an act of the will and to do Satan's work.

Thought and Disease

Sometime ago, I had opportunity to talk with Dr. Jim Winslow, the Director of the City of Faith Medical and Research Center in Tulsa. Dr. Winslow is a surgeon. I asked him a simple question, "How much of the disease that you treat in the hospital has a psychosomatic origin?" He replied, "A conservative estimate would be somewhere between sixty-five and seventy percent."

That is an amazing statistic. It means that most physical afflictions originate in the human mind. The devil is so clever in making this happen.

When I recently applied for life insurance, the doctor called me into his office and began to question me. He went down a list of questions that are commonly asked of anyone making this kind of application: "Do you have any history of cancer in your family?" I began to think about one of my grandmothers who had died because of cancer. I felt fear come upon me like a fist hitting me in my stomach. The doctor went on, "Is there any history of heart disease in your family?" I replied by telling about one of my uncles who had died of a heart attack. The fear inside of me increased.

I didn't realize what was happening until later. Satan was taking a simple, innocent question from a doctor and using it as a thought bomb to attack my mind. That's how he puts disease upon us. He whispers in your mind, "See, it's in your family. Your parents had it, your grandparents had it, your relatives had it, so you are going to get it too." He conditions us to receive disease through manipulation and suggestion in the area of our thoughts. The diabolically clever reasoning behind it is so subtle. It may be a perfectly innocent question from a doctor—one that is asked to everyone—and yet what it triggers inside of us is awesome in its impact.

In my crusade services around the country, I meet so many people who are living under the haunting terror of inherited disease. When I expose this tool of the devil in controlling their minds, many people are set free from the bondage of the enemy. That is why praise and worship are such powerful means for redirecting the thoughts of our minds toward the Lord instead of upon the disease that Satan wants us to focus on.

This book is designed to show you how to handle those thoughts, to show you how to tear down the strongholds of the devil, to show you how to come into a tremendous faith for healing and deliverance, to show you how to receive revelation from God, to show you that the weapons of your warfare are mighty through God to pull down the strongholds of the devil.

It is my conviction that such spiritual understanding will enable you to realize tremendous power and victory in your life. Our greatest need is to appropriate the truth that Satan is a defeated foe, to believe it and apply it to our lives.

As you read these pages, a tremendous faith is going to build up on the inside of you—faith to pull down the strongholds of Satan's thought. That faith will be released by the process of praise. You will find yourself moving into signs and wonders and miracles from God. The following chapters will show you how to make this happen.

2

Weapons of War

How the Kingdom of Darkness Operates

In order to develop an effective strategy for overcoming the suggestions of the devil in the realm of our thoughts, we must have an understanding of how his kingdom operates. It is absolutely essential for us to understand the Scriptural basis through which we can experience victory. The veil that darkens our minds must be pulled aside. How Satan operates in his kingdom—where he operates from—must be exposed. In other words, *we need to grasp the full scenario of spiritual warfare,* and understand its ramifications.

Paul writes in 2 Corinthians 10:3-5:

> **3 For though we walk in the flesh, we do not war after the flesh:**
> **4 (For the weapons of our warfare are not carnal, but mighty through God to the pulling down of strong holds;)**
> **5 Casting down imaginations, and every high thing that exalteth itself against the knowledge of God, and bringing into captivity every thought to the obedience of Christ.**

Strongholds

Verse 4 of this text identifies the source of the attack against you and me. Paul identifies the evil spiritual personalities who try to bind us. He calls them "strongholds." This passage provides us with the only place in the New Testament where the word "strongholds" may be found. What does this important and distinctive word mean? Strongholds consist of anything evil used by the devil to bind you in any area of your life. Disease may be a stronghold. Satanic oppression in the mind is a stronghold. There may be strongholds in your marriage, in your family relationships. Temptation is a stronghold. Financial bondage is a stronghold. In spite of these strongholds, Paul tells us that the weapons of our warfare are mighty—"to the pulling down of strong holds." Praise the Lord!

Notice the effective imagery Paul uses. What does he mean, for example, by "the pulling **down** of strong holds"? A consistent theme in Paul's epistles concerns the location of Satan's realm. Satan is called "the prince of the power of the air." "For we wrestle not against flesh and blood, but against principalities, against powers,..." The end of this verse locates the satanic realm as being "...in high places" (Eph. 6:12).

The Greek word from which "high places" is translated is **epouranios.** This word appears in four additional places in the book of Ephesians: Eph. 1:3, 1:20, 2:6, and 3:10. Each of these references uses the translation: "heavenly places." The immensity of what Paul was trying to communicate about Satan's realm must have been difficult for the translators of the King James version to comprehend; therefore, they chose to use "high places" instead of "heavenly places" in Ephesians 6:12.

Most people believe the devil lives in hell. This is not correct. **The Scriptures teach, very conclusively, that the devil actually lives in heaven.** This, however, is not the same heaven where God dwells. In Old Testament Hebrew the word for "heaven" is **shemaim,** and in the New Testament

Greek one of the words is **epouranios.** Both of these words are **plural,** indicating the existence of more than one heaven.

Several Heavens

The first verse of the Bible says, "In the beginning God created the heaven and the earth." Heaven (**shemaim**) is a plural word. There are several heavens. Paul writes in 2 Corinthians 12:2, 4:

> **2 I knew a man in Christ above fourteen years ago, (whether in the body, I cannot tell; or whether out of the body, I cannot tell: God knoweth;) such an one caught up to the *third heaven...***
> **4 How that he was caught up into paradise, and heard unspeakable words, which it is not lawful for a man to utter.**

Paul is describing the presence of God in paradise. Clearly God dwells in "the third heaven."

Since there is a third heaven, there must be first and second heavens also. Psalms 19:1 reveals, "The heavens declare the glory of God; and the firmament sheweth his handywork." The universe, as we know it, forms the first "heaven." There are only oblique references in the Scriptures to a "second heaven." One of these is found in Revelation 14:6: "And I saw another angel fly in the midst of heaven..." In Greek, the word "midst" is a single compound noun. It could be variously translated as "the mid-heaven" or "middle heaven."

In the book of the Revelation, John declares, "And there was war in heaven..." (Rev. 12:7). How could there be war in heaven if God dwells there alone? The passage goes on to say in verses 7 and 8:

> **7 ...Michael and his angels fought against the dragon; and the dragon fought and his angels,**
> **8 And prevailed not; neither was their place**

found any more in heaven.

Notice the ending of this verse: "...neither was their place found *any more* in heaven." It appears that up until this point the devil had lived in heaven. The book of the Revelation describes future events. This particular event has not yet transpired. Therefore, it is safe to conclude that the devil presently lives in heaven, but *notice,* he does not live in God's heaven.

When Satan was cast out of the presence of God, he established a command post of his own in an area of the universe known as the second heaven. He works there with principalities, powers, rulers of the darkness, and wicked spirituals. These comprise the strongholds Paul speaks of in 2 Corinthians 10:4. These strongholds have set themselves against you and me, and are masters at controlling the thoughts of mankind.

This is what Jesus referred to in Matthew 16:19 when he said, "And I will give unto thee the keys of the kingdom of heaven: and whatsoever thou shalt bind on earth shall be bound in heaven: and whatsoever thou shalt loose on earth shall be loosed in heaven." Jesus was directing Peter and the disciples to warfare in the heavenlies. There is certainly no reason for us to bind and loose in the third heaven where God dwells. There is great reason for us to bind and loose in the second heaven, however.

Jesus made a powerful declaration to His disciples after His death and resurrection. In Matthew 28:18, 19 He said,

18 ...All power is given unto me in heaven and in earth.
19 Go ye therefore...

Why did Jesus say all power had been given to Him in heaven? He made the heavens. He was God. He is referring here specifically to the second heaven.

Because of the resurrection, He was telling the disciples, He had power in the second heaven. Then He commissioned them to go into the second heaven when He said, "Go ye therefore."

It is important to notice that these strongholds work on different spiritual levels. Some work on you as an individual. Some work on concepts that bind an entire nation or an entire part of the world. Whether we know it or not, all of us are influenced by these corporate thought systems. Political ideologies, philosophies, and false religious beliefs do control vast numbers of people. The power of the media—especially books and newspapers—enhance this control. Such thought systems are able to spread throughout the world in a very short time.

Thought Bombs

These thought systems are actually "thought bombs," because they are weapons used by the enemy to control vast numbers of people. For example, communism is more than an ideology; it is a tremendously powerful stronghold, a "thought bomb," if you will. It is a spiritually based "thought bomb" generated by Satan, and it holds control over the minds and lives of vast numbers of people. Long ago I realized that to be effective in ministering to the communist world, I must take authority over these strongholds and pull them down through the power of my spiritual weapons.

It is crucial for us to be aware that these "thought bombs" can influence both us and our children. **Secular humanism is one such influence that is engineered by the enemy to gain control over our educational system.** Satan's strategy is to condition the thinking of mankind radically through the deceptive teachings and philosophies of many of the world's great thinkers. Men like Kant, Hegel, Marx, Lenin, Freud, Darwin, and others have introduced ideas—thoughts, if you will—that hold sway over vast numbers of people.

Satan has appointed spiritual personalities to superintend the promulgation of these ideas. These evil personalities promote evil thought concepts throughout the earth. It is all part of Satan's cunning war strategy.

The Bible clearly shows that *some strongholds operate in specific geographical areas.* When Gabriel appeared to Daniel he said, "...the prince of the kingdom of Persia withstood me" (Dan. 10:13). A wicked spiritual prince was responsible for, or at least he had the power to influence, the nation of Persia, and this wicked emissary hindered the angel of God from getting to Daniel. That prince was in charge of the thinking of the nation. His responsibility was Persia. At the end of that same chapter, Gabriel said, "I must go back to deal with the prince of Grecia." There was also an evil personality who was responsible for Greece. Greece was the next great world power that would arise under the influence of Alexander the Great.

These strongholds of the devil have an incredible power in the unseen world. Believers need to be instructed about this power. It is also true that evil personalities influence the cities of our nation. A spirit of the occult operates in New Orleans. A spirit of homosexuality has great influence in San Francisco. A spirit of violence can be found in Chicago. Until we have dealt with the authority of these strongholds, we will not have success in evangelizing the people under their influence. This is one of the great keys in evangelism today.

The Weapons of Our Warfare

"...the weapons of our warfare are...mighty through God to the pulling down of strongholds" (2 Cor. 10:4). This raises a basic question: What does Paul mean by "the weapons of our warfare"?

There are many spiritual weapons described in the Scriptures. Most are defensive weapons: the helmet of salvation, the breastplate of righteousness, the shield of faith, shoes prepared for the gospel of peace, a girdle of truth, etc. In 2 Corinthians 10:4, however, Paul describes offensive weapons.

If we are going to fight the devil, **there are three offensive weapons given by God for the Church's use: the Word of God, the Name of Jesus, and the Blood of Jesus.**

Each of these weapons contains innate spiritual power that has great ability for pulling down the strongholds of the enemy. This book focuses on the foremost of these weapons—the Word of God.

The Word of God

When God gave me a revelation of the modus operandi of the devil, it became clear that his method of operation is in the area of thought control. I also began to realize something else, **God's Word contains the thoughts of God.** When you read the Bible, you are dealing with God's thoughts. "For as the heavens are higher than the earth, so are my ways higher than your ways, and my thoughts than your thoughts" (Isa. 55:9).

The Bible says, "For the Word of God is quick, and powerful, and sharper than any twoedged sword, piercing even to the dividing asunder of soul and spirit, and of the joints and marrow, and is a discerner of the thoughts and intents of the heart" (Heb. 4:12). Notice the word "discerner." It literally means "a judge." Therefore, the Word is a judge of our thoughts. If we do not bring our thoughts under the judgment and authority of the Word of God, we open ourselves to the attack of the devil.

We have already noted that "the weapons of our warfare are...mighty...to the pulling down of strong holds" (2 Cor. 10:4). Verse 5 goes on, "Casting down imaginations, and every high thing that exalteth itself against the knowledge of God, and bringing into captivity every thought to the obedience of Christ." This must be the strategy of the believer in overcoming the strongholds of the devil. We must learn how to cast down imaginations, to cast down proud and highly exalted things. We must find a way to bring every thought into captivity to the mind of Christ.

Pulling Down Strongholds

How do we accomplish this? The writer to the Hebrews instructs us that the Word of God is a discerner of our thoughts. It must be the judge of all our thoughts. If we have not subjected our thoughts to the authority of God's Word, we have not learned how to bring every thought into "captivity to the mind of Christ."

The Christian life is a spiritual battle. That battle centers around our need to bring our thoughts under the judgment of God's thoughts. ***This is done by superimposing God's thoughts over Satan's thoughts.*** Satan's thoughts make you sick. Satan's thoughts create divorce, financial bondage, mental oppression. God's thoughts create healing. They create financial prosperity. They create harmony and health in the home. They create freedom and deliverance from the multitudinous bondages of satanic oppression.

It is in doing this that we come into a direct confrontation with the devil. At this point God calls the believer to fight. Paul points out that we don't wrestle with people who have flesh-and-blood bodies. We wrestle with principalities and powers. We wrestle with strongholds.

How do we wrestle? We use our weapons—God's thoughts. We dare to take God's thoughts and bring them against the thoughts of the devil. If we will stand firm, employing God's thoughts, sooner or later they will win over the thoughts that make us sick and oppressed. This is the arena of spiritual conflict. It is something you must *see* in order to put into practice. This seeing involves understanding through the faculties of your spirit. When you fully see and comprehend this spiritual truth, you will be able to apply it to your life, thus enabling you to experience victory.

The Name of Jesus

The Word of God, as we have already stated, contains the thoughts of God. It is important to realize that **the Name of Jesus is the singularly most powerful thought of God in His Word.**

The early church understood the power of the Name of Jesus. For example, Peter addressed the lame man at the gate of the Temple by saying, "Silver and gold have I none, but such as I have give I thee" (Acts 3:6). Peter had something to give the lame man. It wasn't money. It was the Name. Peter knew that Jesus had given him the "power of attorney" to use His Name. So when Peter faced this sickness, he superimposed God's thoughts over the devil's thoughts. He commanded the bondage of the devil to yield to the Name of Jesus.

A quick examination of the Name of Jesus in the book of Acts reveals that **the early church was obsessed with the power inherent in that Name.** That one single thought (the Name of Jesus) permeated the thinking of the entire church. Everywhere believers went, they went with the Name of Jesus on their lips and in their hearts. The Sanhedrin commanded them to stop teaching and preaching in the Name of Jesus (Acts 4), but they went on healing the sick through that sacred Name. Finally they set them before the council. They said in Acts 5:28, "...Did not we straitly command you that ye should not teach in this name? and behold, ye have filled Jerusalem with your doctrine..." What doctrine? **That doctrine was the Name of Jesus.**

God's thought—the Name of Jesus—had penetrated the spirits of the early Christians. They knew disease would have to bow before the power of the Name. They knew they could evangelize the world with the power of the Name.

Philip went down to Samaria (Acts 8) and preached the Name of Jesus. When Paul was converted, he immediately preached the Name of Jesus in the synagogue. It was the Name of Jesus that gave power to the early church. There was power in God's thought. It was the power that the first century believers used to pull down the strongholds of the devil. We can use that all-powerful Name in the same way.

The Blood of Jesus

It is also true that the Blood of Jesus contains the singularly most powerful group of thoughts in the Word of God. The blood of Jesus represents the doctrine of the Atonement. It is the essence of the gospel message. It represents everything Jesus accomplished on the cross for the salvation of mankind. Paul said that he was not ashamed of the gospel, because it is the power of God unto salvation to all who believe.

When we use the term "the Blood," we mean everything that the cross and the gospel represent. What incredible power is found in that group of thoughts. It is the power of God unto salvation. The verb "to be saved" comes from the Greek word **"sozo."** Its use in the New Testament is interesting to note. For example, **sozo** is used with regard to the healing of the woman with the issue of blood. It is also used in reference to the deliverance of the Gadarean demoniac and in the raising of Jairus's daughter. In James 5 it is used when the prayer of faith for the sick is mentioned. The power of God unto salvation is the power of God unto healing, deliverance, the raising of the dead, the meeting of every one of our spiritual, physical and material needs. The Blood represents all of this.

The Bible says that believers "overcame him (the devil) by the blood of the Lamb, and by the word of their testimony" (Rev. 12:11). **They testified to what the Word said that the Blood did for them.** By so doing, they overcame the power of the devil, and all his accusations. Notice that Satan is called "the accuser of the brethren" (Rev. 12:10). He accuses us before God, day and night. He is there right now before the Throne, accusing you to the Father, but the Bible says we overcome him by the Blood of the Lamb. That is exciting. It shows that God wants us to take authority, and He has provided us with an effective means for doing this.

God wants us to cast down the accusations of the devil. God wants us to bring our thoughts into captivity to the mind of Christ. We are to use our spiritual weapons—the Word, the Name, and the Blood—in bringing every thought into captivity. This is the essence of spiritual warfare.

I believe it is certain that the primary place of attack by Satan is found in our minds and thought life. Thousands of thoughts enter our minds and we need to have a strategy for dealing with them. David said, "I will set no wicked thing before my eyes" (Ps. 101:3). He knew the secret of guarding his mind. He also said, "Let the words of my mouth and the meditation of my heart, be acceptable in thy sight, O Lord, my strength, and my redeemer" (Ps. 19:14). The meditations of our hearts—our thought life— must be acceptable to God.

Your thoughts can tell you that you have every disease in the book. Your thoughts can tell you that you are going to die, that you have committed the unpardonable sin and have failed the Lord. **The devil**

will try to convince you that God is bringing you into judgment for your past sins. There is a tremendously fearful torment in this. Our only answer is to put God's thoughts into our mind.

The Word of God has got to speak to us at this point. We must understand one simple fact. It is not God who torments us. It is not God who condemns us. It is not God who sends us fear. It is coming from the devil. God is the one who loves us. He is the one who sent His Son to die for us. He is the one who has made a way of escape, but there comes a time when ***we*** must turn the Word of God against the devil.

Using the Word

This is the key that Jesus used in Matthew 4. The Bible says that Jesus was led by the Spirit, after His baptism, into the wilderness. He was tempted there of the devil for forty days. The devil came to Him and said, "If thou be the Son of God command that these stones be made bread." Notice even in attacking Jesus, Satan attacked with a thought. He tried to get Him to act contrary to the leading of His Father. But Jesus rebuffed Satan and said, "It is written, man shall not live by bread alone but by every word that proceedeth out of the mouth of God."

Then the devil took Him up to Jerusalem and sat Him on the pinnacle of the temple. He said, "Cast thyself down" and he even went so far as to quote Scripture. Did you know the devil probably knows Scripture better than you do? He can quote it expertly at the right time, but always it is in the wrong context. He uses a seed of truth to create a bushel of error. Notice how Jesus answered him. He took up His weapon; He used the Word of God. "It is written again, Thou shalt not tempt the Lord thy God" (verse 7).

The Key to Spiritual Victory

In the third temptation the devil took Him to the

top of a mountain and showed Him all the kingdoms of the world. He said, "All these things will I give thee, if thou wilt fall down and worship me" (verse 9). Jesus responded, "Get thee hence, Satan: for it is written, Thou shalt worship the Lord thy God, and him only shalt thou serve" (verse 10). Notice again, in defeating the devil, Jesus used our primary weapon—the Word of God. He took one of God's thoughts and fired it against the invading thought of the devil. This is the key to spiritual victory. If Jesus knew the success of it, we must learn the success of it as well. We can do it just like He did.

We must begin to get God's thoughts into our minds to fight off the lies of Satan. We absorb His thoughts by constant meditation on His Word. We must unsheath the sword of the Spirit (the Word of God) and fight the devil with it in the Name of Jesus. When the devil says, "You are weak," reply to him with, "I am strong in the Lord and in the power of His might" (see Eph. 6:10). When the devil makes you fear, tell him boldly, "The Lord is my light and my salvation; whom shall I fear? the Lord is the strength of my life; of whom shall I be afraid?" (Ps. 27:1). *Every Christian can defeat the devil and drive out his thoughts with the simple phrase, "It is written."*

The devil hates to hear these words. I have seen demon spirits loose their control over someone when I quoted the Word of God to them. They know I know that Word. They know if I really believe it. They also know that if I truly believe the Word, then they must be subject to what that Word says. Satan had to acknowledge the authority of God's Word in the wilderness. Demons will be subject to God's Word right now in your life. When the devil tries to overwhelm you with his thoughts, bring out the Word and fight him with it.

Psalm 91 is a great declaration for all believers.

When I read it devotionally, I like to rephrase it in the first person. This personalizes its truth to me.

> "I dwell in the secret place of the most High and I abide under the shadow of the Almighty. I will say of the Lord, He is my refuge and my fortress: my God; in Him will I trust. Surely, He has delivered me from the snare of the fowler, and from the noisome pestilence. He shall cover me with his feathers, and under his wings shall I trust; his truth shall be my shield and buckler.
>
> I will not be afraid for the terror by night; nor for the arrow that flieth by day; nor for the pestilence that walketh in darkness; nor for the destruction that wasteth at noonday. A thousand shall fall at my side, and ten thousand at my right hand; but it shall not come nigh me.
>
> Only with mine eyes shall I behold and see the reward of the wicked. Because I have made the Lord which is my refuge, even the most High, my habitation; no evil shall befall me, neither shall any plague come nigh my dwelling because he has given his angels charge over me and all my household."

You can do the same through the important process of personalizing the Scriptures.

God's angels are watching over me. Praise the Lord! God's angels are waiting for me to use the Word against the devil. Jesus is the High Priest of my confession. He waits for me to bring the Word against the devil. What a powerful position God has given us through the weapons of our warfare. When you see this your life will be changed.

I have seen Christians endure violent attacks in their minds and bodies. I have seen believers go to the hospital because of a thought. The doctors have said there is nothing more they can do. There is a deep, deep darkness that covers them. They scream out in terror. Their thoughts are under the grip and control of the devil. They have been made his captives. The devil tells them that their loving heavenly Father was the one who created this sickness. He tells them they must suffer patiently. *What a lie! This is a stronghold of the devil.* If you listen to his thoughts long enough, if you meditate on them—sooner or later you will begin to say with your mouth what Satan has said in your mind.

Our Mouths—The Center of Spiritual Warfare

I am convinced that the mouth is the center of spiritual warfare for the universe. The devil is after your mouth, and God is after your mouth. This explains why, in the baptism of the Holy Spirit, God utilizes your mouth through speaking in tongues. When we pray in the spirit, we are declaring the wonderful works of God. We are entering into the act of praise and worship.

Praying in the spirit becomes an act of spiritual warfare. It fills your spirit with the thoughts of God. It prepares your mind to receive the thoughts of God. In fact, one of the most successful means of renewing the mind is to pray in the spirit. It makes you immediately sensitive to the thoughts of God. When His thoughts come into your mind they have great power. This is the key to revelation. This is what sets you free.

Soviet Confrontation

My ministry would be helpless if it were not for God's thoughts. Over the years I have learned to seek after and treasure those thoughts. Let me illustrate what I mean. In 1979 I was preaching in Bath, England. The Spirit of the Lord moved on me in the middle of my message. I received one of God's thoughts.

I stopped preaching and turned to my European director, Mike McKibben. I said, "Mike, the Spirit of the Lord is telling me that we will be in the Soviet Union in one month. We are to take in a recording studio for the underground church." This was a shocking announcement especially in light of the fact that it seemed impossible to organize everything that quickly. Also, we didn't have the money to buy the equipment for the recording studio. We needed about $40,000.

Several days later a man came to our European office in Malmesbury, England. He brought a check with him for close to $40,000. We had never met him before. That was the first miracle. Our visas were granted immediately by the Soviet government. That was the second miracle. One month later we were ready to go.

I flew into West Berlin in the month of October to join the team. On the way to my hotel, the team leader, Randy Innes, informed me that he had taken delivery of some lead printing plates of the Bible. Someone had asked us to take them into the Soviet Union. I realized immediately the severe consequences of this action but I promised Randy I would pray about it. That night in prayer I became aware that we were to take the equipment in.

The next night at 10:30 we pulled up to the Soviet border. The team members were not aware of the lead printing plates nor of the fact that we had taped them to the inside of the monitor speakers. The Soviet guards demanded that everything be taken off our bus so they could examine it. One of our young men, Gary, lifted the monitor speaker and groaned out loud. "Whatever is in here?" he exclaimed. "These speakers never weighed this much before." My heart sank when the Soviet guard walked over with his cane and tapped on the outside of the speaker box." What is in here?" he asked.

Someone went to get a screw driver to open the case. I stood there praying in the Spirit and saying to the Lord, "Father, I know that you impressed me to do this during my prayer time last night." When they came back with the screw driver the guard said, "Open this box instead." He pointed to another speaker. They opened it. There was nothing in it except the speaker. I breathed a prayer of thanksgiving to the Lord.

The next day we were scheduled to sing at a Baptist church on the outskirts of Kiev. When we arrived a large group of young people gathered around our bus to greet us. A young woman whispered in my ear that an underground church leader had driven many hundreds of miles to meet me and was waiting about one half mile from the church out in the forest. I followed her. I met the brother whom I had known for some time. We prayed together and discussed our itinerary. I heard music coming from the church and realized it was time for the meeting to begin.

I walked back through the forest toward the church. When I stepped out of the bush I stopped. I saw a police militia van (a paddy wagon) in front of our bus. There were eight policemen sitting in the van. They all saw me as I stepped out of the bush. The first thought that crossed my mind was, "They have arrested the members of the group and they are now waiting for me." I crossed the road and got on our bus. They drove their van back down the road in the direction from which I had come.

I quickly made my way into the church. The building was crowded with people. I sat down by our underground interpreter, Viktor. He said, "They're here tonight." I queried, "Who is here?" He said, "The Soviet secret police, the KGB."

Sure enough, when it came time for me to bring greetings to the crowd, the secret police stood in front of me with cameras and flash bulbs popping. One man held up a microphone to document everything I was saying. The drummer for our group went outside during my talk. A man approached him speaking in fluent American English. "We know who you are," he said, "We know that you have been here before. We will not allow you to get away with what you did last time. We will stop you."

When I returned to my hotel that night I knew we were going to have a direct confrontation with Soviet authorities. I also knew that the lives of four-teen young people were in my hands. My decisions would directly affect them. It could mean imprison-ment for us all. More than anything else, I needed to know God's thoughts.

I knelt by my bed and started to pray in my prayer language. I knew this was the best way for me to prepare myself to hear God's thoughts. I started at 10:30 P.M. One hour passed by—nothing—two hours, three hours. Finally, six hours later at 4:30 A.M. one thought began to reoccur in my mind, **Acts chapter four.**

I took out my New Testament and began to read. Peter and John were threatened by the high priests. They were told not to preach in Jesus' Name. Their answer in verse 19 came alive inside of me."But Peter and John answered and said unto them, Whether it be right in the sight of God to hear-ken unto you more than unto God, judge ye. For we cannot but speak the things which we have seen and heard."

I knew I had my answer. I had received God's thought. I was to be bold and declare the Word of the Lord. He would take care of the consequences.

The next morning, I joined the team for break-fast. Our Soviet guide, Igor, came to the breakfast table. "Terry, there are some men here who want to talk to you," he said. I went with him to a special room in the hotel. They had prepared it for interrogation.

I sat down in front of a large desk. Behind the desk was a man in a military uniform. A woman interpreter sat beside the desk. A man, who I surmised to be a KGB agent, sat on a chair in the corner watching me closely.

The man behind the desk spoke loudly, "You have broken our laws," he said. "You have gone to a church without official permission. When you are in the Soviet Union, you will obey our instructions. You will only be allowed to go where your itinerary states." He continued in this vein for twenty minutes, adding that they were considering putting me in prison.

As I listened, the words of Acts Chapter 4 came back to me. I knew I was to speak boldly and leave the consequences to God. I held up my hand. "Do you have something to say?" he questioned.

To this day, I don't recall where I learned what I said to the man. I must have read it in their literature somewhere. I began to quote the Soviet constitution.

I said, "Sir, according to the new Soviet Constitution ratified in 1977, Article 52 declares that you have freedom of religion in the U.S.S.R. Is that correct?" He was shocked. "Yes, that is correct," he said.

"I believe that because I am a tourist in your country I am protected by the laws of your constitution. Is that correct?" I asked.

"Yes, that is correct," he said.

"In view of that, we have come to the Soviet Union to exercise our freedom of religion," I said. "Our right to do so is guaranteed by your law."

The man sitting on the chair in the corner became quite agitated. He got up and came over to me. "You will not be allowed to meddle with our domestic affairs," he shouted.

I replied, "Sir, we have told you why we are here. The gospel says that God so loved the world He gave His only begotten Son." I began to explain the gospel to him. Then I stood up and said, "Gentlemen, we have nothing to hide. Do with us what you will." Quietly I left the room (and died of a heart attack in the hall outside). I was literally trembling from head to toe. But I knew one thing—God's thought had given me a boldness beyond myself. It had confounded their interrogation techniques. Without God's thoughts, my friend, we are nothing.

The Believer's Launching Rockets

So far I have told you that there are strongholds that dwell in the second heaven. Jesus said, "Whatever you bind on earth will be bound in heaven" (the second heaven). How is it possible for us to use our ability to bind in the second heaven? How can we get our weapons into the second heaven to attack the power of strongholds? How can we superimpose the power of our weapons over the power of the thoughts of the devil? We need a delivery system that will get our weapons into the second heaven.

There are four spiritual launching rockets that God has provided for us.

Prayer

The first one is *prayer.* Prayer does not have power in and of itself. Jesus said the heathen pray with vain repetitions, but God doesn't listen. There is no power in that kind of praying. The key to the power in prayer resides in the weapon that prayer carries. The power of prayer is in the Word, the Name, and the Blood. How much of the Word are you praying? How much of the Name are you praying? How much of the Blood are you praying?

Prayer is a launching rocket. It focuses the attack on the devil. It carries your weapon to the point of attack. You can pray for someone in a Soviet concentration camp and bring the power of God, through the Word, into the middle of that concentration camp.

Prayer is the conveyor of power. It's like a rocket. In nuclear warfare, the power to destroy is in the nuclear warhead the rocket carries. The power of God to destroy the strongholds of the devil is in the Word, the Name, and the Blood. Therefore, our launching rockets must carry the Word to the point of attack. When you understand prayer in this context, it will change your praying. It will give power to your prayers. It will give you new authority.

Preaching

The second launching rocket is **preaching.** Every time I stand up to preach the Word of God, I declare to the strongholds in my audience that I have authority over them through the Scriptures. That's why Paul said to Timothy, "Preach the word" (2 Tim. 4:2). Paul knew that the power of preaching was not in the preaching itself. It was in the weapon the preaching carried. The power of preaching is in the Word, not in my preaching gift or in my oratory. I know if I preach the Word, people will be set free. People will be healed. People will be delivered. Therefore, it is my task to preach the Word.

It is also my task (in this book) to get the Word into you. As I deliver the Word to you, an anointing comes with it. I am sending out a weapon. *This word is smashing the devil's thought systems that have you bound. You can be healed at this very moment, as you read these words.* This is God's thought coming to you. There is an energy, power, and life in this thought of God. It has greater power than the power of sickness that binds your body.

Preaching therefore, must focus on the Word, the Name, and the Blood. The more of these three weapons we get into our preaching, the more power we will have in our preaching. We will see more miracles happen in the lives of the people in our audience. When I preach against strongholds in my meetings, they are forced to bow. People are healed instantaneously as they hear the Word preached. Preaching is a launching rocket. It carries the Word, the Name, and the Blood into the hearts of God's people and into the hearts of the unsaved.

Testimony

The third launching rocket is **testimony** or **witness.** The Bible says, "But ye shall receive power, after that the Holy Ghost is come upon you: and ye shall be witnesses unto me both in Jerusalem, and in all Judaea, and in Samaria, and unto the uttermost part of the earth" (Acts 1:8). These were the last words spoken by Jesus on the earth. In the next verse, He ascended to heaven. He announced to His disciples the coming of the **Paracletos**—the Holy Spirit. He said that when He came they would receive power. That word "power" in the Greek is **"dunamis"** from which we get words like dynamite, dynamo and dynamic. You shall receive **spiritual dynamite.**

What will we do with the power? Will we talk in tongues? That's not what He said. Will we form a denomination that separates us from the Body of Christ? That's not what He said. Will we form little "bless me" clubs, where we get together to be emotionally uplifted? That's not what Jesus said. He said, "ye shall receive power," and "ye shall be witnesses unto me." **The bottom line of the baptism of the Holy Spirit is the power to be a witness.**

You have the power of God anointing you to be a witness if you are baptized in the Holy Spirit. You don't have to wait for God to make you a witness or for God to "prompt" you to witness, you have the anointing to do it any time. But notice how the devil has the church tied up with thought bombs. He's made people terrified to share their testimony. He has put fear into their hearts. He has attacked their minds and told them that others will laugh at them—that others will not receive their testimony. Satan has bound up the immense and awesome power of the Holy Spirit inside of you with one simple little thought—*fear.*

Do you see what this has done on a massive scale? The devil has incapacitated the church. He has robbed it of this incredibly powerful launching rocket, and he does it by making you afraid. He may say, "What if it doesn't work? You're not an expert at doing it. You're not a preacher. You haven't studied in Bible college. They are going to laugh at your testimony." We listen and begin to think those thoughts are ours. We receive them from the devil and consequently allow him to bottle up this launching rocket of God. If the Church of Jesus Christ were to see this truth and release the tremendous power of the Holy Spirit within them, through their witness and testimony, *we would evangelize the world within a few years.*

Praise and Worship

The next launching rocket is praise and worship. *There is an awesome power in praise and worship that is relatively unrecognized in the church today.* Paul and Silas were in a Philippian prison. They had been beaten by the rulers of the people. Their whips had been laid upon their backs. Their feet were in bonds. I am sure their bodies ached; searing pain must have penetrated every part of their beings.

What does a man like Paul do when he faces the devil? It's one thing to teach a church—it's one thing to write a book that says your weapons are mighty, but what does he do when he faces the devil. It is interesting to notice how Paul put his weapons into action.

The Bible says in Acts 16: 25, 26:

25 *And at midnight* **Paul and Silas prayed, and sang praises unto God: and the prisoners heard them** (italics mine).
26 And suddenly there was a great earthquake...

Paul knew how to use his weapons. He knew how to get them into action. He and Silas sang praises to the Lord. They uplifted the power of the Lord's Name. The Name was the weapon they used in that Philippian jail, but the vehicle, or the rocket, that carried that Name was the power of praise. Notice how the foundations of the prison were shaken! There was a great earthquake.

You may be in the midnight of disease. You may be in the nightmare of satanic oppression with fear and doubt. You may be going through a divorce in your family. The devil may have your finances tied up. You may be encountering an incredibly powerful temptation. It may be midnight in your life. But notice what Paul and Silas did at midnight: *they sang praises.* Praise is the launching rocket. Praise releases the power of God in your spirit and moves you into a position of attack against the devil's thoughts.

Each of the four launching rockets is exercised by an individual. You pray, preach, witness, and praise individually. You've got to do it yourself.

Praise and worship have a corporate dimension as well as an individual one. When we come together with the Body of Christ—regardless of our numbers— we have the incredible opportunity of entering into united power in the launching of a spiritual rocket. We immediately invoke the law of spiritual agreement. The Bible says, "One man shall put a thousand to flight, two men—ten thousand" (Deut. 32:30, my paraphrase). Notice what this geometric progression suggests: three could put 100,000 to flight, and so on.

When a thousand people lift their voices in praise to God, there is so much spiritual energy generated that it literally begins to knock and shake the power of strongholds in the second heaven. That's why people in my meetings are healed. In the midst of praise and worship, blind eyes are opened, deaf ears are unstopped—there is a singular manifestation of divine power. Why? Because tremendous faith is released by the launching rocket of praise and worship.

I focus the faith of the people on the launching of a weapon—the Word, the Name, and the Blood— we use praise to launch the weapon. As we do it together, we pull down strongholds. It always works. In the process, many thousands of people are saved, healed and delivered.

3

The Powerful Word

The Word, Our Weapon

When a young man goes into the army, one of the first things he learns is how to use a weapon. They put a rifle in his hands. They teach him how to dismantle it. They even teach him how to do it while blindfolded. After his training, he can take his weapon apart and put it back together in the middle of the night during a hurricane, if need be. He's also taught how to fire his weapon with accuracy.

In the army of God, the same kind of skill is needed. We need to become familiar with our weapons. **In this chapter I want to focus on the power of one particular weapon—the Word of God.** Let's examine it thoroughly, and become acquainted with this great weapon God has put in our hands.

Some of what you will read on the following pages will be new to you. Certain things may even surprise you. The goal is to prepare you for victory.

The phrase, "the Word of God" is very important. It refers, of course, to the Bible. However, it also is used to refer to Jesus Christ Himself. John 1:1 says, "In the beginning was the Word, and the Word was with God and the Word was God." The same chapter goes on, "And the Word was made flesh and dwelt among us" (John 1:14). This raises an obvious question. **What, or who, is the Word of God?** Is the Word of God, Jesus, or is it the Bible?

When the Scripture calls itself the Word of God, and when the Bible calls Jesus Himself the Word of God, God is speaking of the unity inherent in their natures. **Both the Bible and Christ are the Word of God.** Each alike is a revelation of God Himself. They agree with each other. There is a unity between them. They contain the divine nature of God (Zoe) in different manifestations. The Bible contains the written Word of God; Christ is the living Word of God. Jesus is a perfect representation and fulfillment of the Bible.

Most believers know that they became Christians by believing in Christ. They don't have a problem with that fact. It's basic to our understanding of the doctrine of salvation. However, most believers have never seen that their relationship to Christ will be the same as their relationship to the Scriptures. They must believe in the Bible as much as they believe in Christ because the two are one. You don't love God anymore than you love His Word. Your love for the Word is the barometer of your love for God.

Seeing Jesus

In John 14, we see an interesting dialogue between Jesus and His disciples. Jesus has told them that He is about to be taken away from them. They don't understand what He's talking about. Jesus says, "Yet a little while, and the world seeth me no more; but ye see me..." (John 14:19). An alternate rendering of His statement could be, "but ye shall continue to see me." Judas answers, "Lord, how is it that thou wilt manifest thyself unto us, and not unto the world? (John 14:22). In effect, he asked, "Lord, if you are here and we can see you, why won't everybody else be able to see you? What kind of communication system is there going to be between you and us?"

Jesus answered, "If a man love me, he will keep my words: and my Father will love him, and we will come unto him, and make our abode with him" (John 14:23).

Jesus gives us a tremendous key in this verse. All of us need to grasp this spiritual truth. Jesus said, "If a man loves me, he will **keep** my words." That word "keep" is an old English term that means **doing** God's Word. If we love Jesus, we will **do** His words. We will put His words into action. We will say to the devil, "It is written." We will launch our weapons with our launching rockets.

Judas asked the question this way, "Lord, how will you manifest yourself to us?" Jesus answered, "If you do my words, both the Father and I will come to you and we will make our home [abode] with you."

There are four principles in this statement that are important for us to see. The first is doing God's Word which makes us different as believers. Secondly, doing God's Word shows that we love Him and God loves us in return. The third principle is that by doing the Word of God Jesus will manifest Himself to us. The fourth principle is that when we do the Word, both the Father and the Son come into our lives and establish an everlasting home in our hearts. *Notice the key is always found in doing the Word.*

Doing the Word

Doing God's Word lets the world know you are a believer. The degree to which you put the Word into practice indicates how much you love God. *As you do His Word, Christ will manifest Himself to you.* That's how God the Father and His Son, Jesus, come into your life.

These facts carry awesome implications for the believer's life. Your attitude toward God's Word is your attitude toward God Himself. You may make lofty declarations concerning your love for God, but the amount of time and devotion you give to His Word represent how much you love Him. *You don't love God in greater degree than you love His Word.*

You don't honor God more than you honor His Word. This is a very simple measuring stick: if you want to know how much God means to you, examine how much His Word means to you. How much time do you give to it daily? Have you committed your heart to *doing* that Word, rather than just *hearing* it? This is the key.

In Matthew 7:24-27, we read these words:

24 Therefore whosoever heareth these sayings of mine, and doeth them, I will liken him unto a wise man, which built his house upon a rock:
25 And the rain descended, and the floods came, and the winds blew, and beat upon that house; and it fell not: for it was founded upon a rock.
26 And every one that heareth these sayings of mine, and doeth them not, shall be likened unto a foolish man, which built his house upon the sand:
27 And the rain descended, and the floods came, and the winds blew, and beat upon that house; and it fell: and great was the fall of it.

In this parable both houses were attacked—the rains descended, the floods came, and the winds blew.

When you become a Christian, the floods will come, the rain will descend, and the winds will blow. That's guaranteed. Why did one house stand and the other fall? The Bible says the difference was found in their foundations. One foundation was built on rock and the other on sand.

What does it mean to build our house upon a rock? Perhaps we have become too familiar with this story. We may have sung it as a Sunday school chorus, but have we ever caught the impact of what Jesus is saying? Both men in the story heard the sayings of Jesus; the difference was found in the doing of them. The man with his house on the rock heard the Word and did it. The man with his house on the sand heard the same Word but he didn't do it. That is the difference. Both of these men attend your church, by the way. Which one are you?

I know believers who have heard the Word for the last twenty or thirty years. Doctrinely, they believe they can be healed. Doctrinely, they believe God wants to bless them. Doctrinely, they believe they can be set free from the oppression of evil spirits. But they have never determined literally to **do** the Word. They've never made up their mind to get healed.

Learning the Principle

Several years ago I experienced an overwhelming tragedy in my life. I was awakened in the night over in England and told that my late wife had been killed in a car accident. I thought my ministry was over. I complained bitterly to the Lord. I mentioned all of my spiritual "brownie" points to Him. I said, "This is not fair."

About a month after the funeral I had opportunity to talk to Oral Roberts. We were in his office. We talked about death and sorrow and how to respond to it. At the end of the conversation, he stood up and said, "Young man, I'm going to tell you something that will save your life, if you will do what I say. I want you to go home, go before the Lord and start to pray in your prayer language. I want you to praise the Lord in the midst of your adverse circumstance."

When he said this, I knew that this was the Word of the Lord coming to me. I knew I had to become a doer of God's Word. The next morning before daybreak I got up and knelt by my bed. I had determined to praise the Lord. I said, "Hallelujah." It was as though the devil whispered in my ear and said, "What are you praising God for, Terry Law. Your wife is dead."

I said more words, "Thank you, Jesus."

The devil said, "How can you praise the Lord when you have three little children without a mother. You don't mean those words. You are a hypocrite."

After fifteen minutes of this kind of spiritual battle I was ready to quit. There was a dark spiritual oppression overwhelming my spirit. I was saying to the Lord, "Father, it is too hard to be a doer of your Word. It is not working."

Then I sensed the words of the psalmist David coming up out of my spirit. Psalm 34:1, "I will bless the Lord at all times; his praise shall continually be in my mouth." I was like a drowning man looking for a lifesaver. I clung onto David's words. I made a decision. I said to myself, "I will bless the Lord at all times; His praise shall be in my mouth right now." I set my jaw and continued to praise the Lord. It was almost two and a half hours before I *felt* anything. The devil laughed at me all this time. I knew I had to be a doer of the Word.

After two and a half hours something broke loose inside of me. I began to pray in the spirit and interpret back to myself in English. I commanded the bitterness, the self-pity, the anger, to get out of my life. When I got up off of my knees several hours later, I was healed. I praised the Lord like this daily for two months.

One day, sometime later, the Lord spoke to me in my bedroom and said, *"If you will lead people into my presence through praise and worship, I will heal the sick, save the lost and deliver the oppressed."* I immediately called my office and informed our music director, Don Moen, of God's instruction. We were going to begin a ministry of healing and deliverance based on praise to the Lord.

Now please understand, I didn't know any other evangelist who was bringing healing to the sick through praise. This was God's Word to me and I had to be a doer of that Word. We scheduled our first praise and healing crusade in Woodward, Oklahoma, in February, 1983. When we arrived in town, Woodward was experiencing a bad snowstorm. I felt that no one would come to our meeting. There were approximately seventy to eighty people who showed up. I told them what the Lord had told me. "We are going to see God heal the sick tonight in the midst of our praise," I declared.

I knew it must have sounded bold to the audience but I didn't feel very bold when I said it. After my message on praise, I began to pray for the sick. I commanded disease to leave sick bodies. I felt so weak and helpless. The devil continued to mock me saying, "Nobody is being healed. When you ask the people if God has touched them, you are going to look foolish." I asked the question, "Has God healed anyone?" Seven people raised their hands. From that moment to this, I have never conducted a healing service without someone being healed. The key that the Lord revealed to me was—***You must be a doer of the Word.***

Only when you ***do*** the Word are you able to do what Jesus did in the wilderness. Only then can you say, "Satan, it is written." You can then attack disease with the Word of God. You can then superimpose God's thoughts over the thoughts of the devil. Only when you do this can you know that you have built your house upon the rock.

There is a vast difference between hearing and doing. This is the major dividing point in most churches today. James 1:22-24 says:

22 ...be ye doers of the word, and not hearers only, deceiving your own selves..
23 For if any be a hearer of the word, and not a doer, he is like unto a man beholding his natural face in a glass:
24 For he beholdeth himself, and goeth his way, and straightway forgetteth what manner of man he was.

In this passage James describes what happens in many of our churches on Sunday mornings. The pastor preaches the Word of God. The congregation hears it. They become hearers of the Word, but if they do not commit themselves to **do** that Word, they become like a man who looks at himself in a mirror. The Word is a mirror. It shows us what we are. It reveals our sin, our mistakes, our problems. It also reveals the fact of our righteousness and blessing.

The problem is not in the Word. **The problem is found in how we respond to it.** If we are hearers only and not doers, we build our houses on the sand. When the trials of life come, when the devil puts on the pressure, when inflation hits the economy, when the devil attacks on the job, our house will fall. When the banker says you're not going to be able to pay your bills, your house falls. If you've not been a doer of the Word, you're going to fall.

Building on the Rock

Jesus showed us how to build on the rock. "Whosoever heareth these saying of mine and **doeth them**." That is the key to victory.

If we are going to **do** the Word—if we are going to make that ultimate commitment, we must understand something about the Word itself. We must make a basic decision about the Word. **The truth about its nature must penetrate our spirits.** What does God's Word say about itself?

Hebrews 4:12 contains an enlightening message, "For the word of God is quick, and powerful, and sharper than any twoedged sword, piercing even to the dividing asunder of soul and spirit, and of the joints and marrow, and is a discerner of the thoughts and intents of the heart." The first phrase tells us that the Word of God is quick and powerful. The Greek word for "quick" simply means "alive." The Word of God is **alive.** Do you believe the Scripture is alive just like Jesus is alive?

The Greek word for powerful is "**energes**." It is the root word for our English word "energetic." The writer to the Hebrews says the Word of God is **alive** and it is **energetic.** Let's meditate on that statement for a moment. The Bible is full of intense, vibrant energy and life. Jesus said the same thing in John 6:63, "...the words that I speak unto you, they are spirit, and they are life." What a fantastic proclamation Jesus makes here. He points out that there is spirit in His words, there is life in His words. When we deal with a promise of God in the Scriptures we are dealing with the very life of Jesus. His thoughts carry His life (divine nature). His thoughts carry His spirit.

In 1 Thessalonians 2:13 we read, "For this cause also thank we God without ceasing, because, when ye received the word of God which ye heard of us, ye received it not as the word of men, but as it is in truth, the word of God, which effectually worketh also in you that believe." Paul is writing here about the Word of God: "This word of God effectually worketh in you that believe." There is a basic truth revealed in these two verses that is fundamental to the action of your faith: until you truly believe that there is spirit and life in God's Word, you'll never really want to do it. Until you understand that there is a vibrant energy and activity in the Word of God, it will never be more to you than just a book. God's Word is life. It is alive. It is energetic. It works!

The Word of God Works

Paul taught that the Word of God **works** in you.
Do you believe that? **Do you believe God's Word
works in you?** Will God's Word work against your
disease? Will it work against your divorce? Will it
work against your financial bondage? Do you believe
it will?

There is only one thing that governs the degree
to which the Word of God can work. That is our
reaction to the Word. "Wherefore lay apart all filthiness and superfluity of naughtiness, and receive with
meekness the engrafted word, which is able to save
your souls" (James 1:21). Before we truly hear the
Word of God, there are two things we must lay aside:
filthiness and naughtiness.

What is meant by filthiness? This term indicates
an excitement over anything that is impure or wicked.
This kind of attitude closes you off to the truth of
God's Word. Naughtiness is a term we usually em-
ploy to refer to a child who is being bad. A typical
characteristic of a child is to do its own thing. It
doesn't want to listen to its parents. It doesn't want
to be obedient to their instruction. It answers back.
It wants to go its own way. There is a root of rebellion in the child.

The unregenerate mind does not want to submit
itself to the Word of God. When you are saved, your
spirit is regenerated. It's recreated, but your mind
also needs to be renewed. Your mind remains unregenerate; it remains in rebellion against the Word of
God. It does not want to submit itself to God's Word
and that is why so many of us are hindered in the
doing of God's Word. God's Word won't work for us
if we continue in a spirit of rebellion. We must make
our minds submit to the Lordship of God's Word. We
must make our thoughts agree with God's thoughts.

It is interesting to observe how people respond to the Word. Several people can sit side by side in a service and only one will respond to the Word of God by doing it and receiving a miracle. Someone else will hear it and say, "I've heard it before and I've never seen anything happen so why should I believe something is going to happen now." Consequently, nothing does happen. **Our reaction to the Word determines its working.** It won't work if our reaction to it is wrong. The Word of God is full of energy. It's full of life. It's full of healing. It's full of financial blessing. It's full of deliverance from oppressing spirits, but your reaction to the Word determines its action in you. That's why Jesus said we must be doers of the Word and not hearers only.

The Word is a Sword

A two-edged sword was used by Roman soldiers. The Roman Empire was established through this weapon being used in the hands of its soldiers. It was a great tool for fighting, but the writer of Hebrews says that the Word of God is sharper than that famous two-edged Roman sword. It pierces "to the dividing asunder of soul and spirit, and of the joints and marrow." This Word divides people into two groups: those who are hearers and those who are doers. Those who receive the Word of God are saved, healed, and prospered. Those who hear it and don't do it are lost.

The Word can set family members against each other. Jesus said in Matthew 10:34, 35:

34 ...I came not to send peace, but a sword.
35 For I am come to set a man at variance against his father, and the daughter against her mother...

There is something about the Word of God that separates even members of the same household—those who are hearers and those who are doers. The *[handwritten: 2 reactions hearing or doing in the (crossed out), in the Spirit / mind / which one]*

hearers are always going to criticize the doers. It is important that the doers do not return the criticism.

There are many today who have seen the truth of doing the Word of God and have become spiritually proud. They criticize those who are hearers only. Spiritual pride of this sort can be communicated from the pulpit very easily. If we are truly doers of the Word, then we will manifest the love of Christ by encouraging our brethren who have not seen the power of this truth. We will lift them up. We will seek to emphasize the truth so that they can see it too, so that they can receive their healing, so that their lives can be turned around by the energy of God's Word.

Here Comes the Judge

Notice the final phrase in Hebrews 4:12—"For the word of God is quick, and powerful...and is a discerner (or a judge) of the thoughts and intents of the heart." This is an important key. First of all, we must understand that the Word of God is alive. It is energetic and it works. Then we must understand that it pierces to the dividing asunder of the two reactions— hearing and doing. **Hearing is in the mind. Doing is in the Spirit.**

The Word forces us to react in one way or the other. When we hear it, we decide whether we will **do** it. When we decide to do it the Word becomes a judge of the thoughts and intents of our hearts. When you receive revelation concerning the character of God's Word—when you commit yourself to doing it, then you are called into action. The action you take is to make God's Word the judge of your thoughts. You're the one who does this.

It is your responsibility, in renewing your mind, to bring the thoughts of God into action against the thoughts of the devil. That is why the praise and worship message that God has led me into, is so important. When we praise the Lord and use the weapon of the Word, when we sing one of the Psalms, we bring that Psalm into action in our lives. When we sing a simple verse such as, "I am the God that healeth thee, Jehovah Rapha," when we praise God with that truth in our spirits, we bring God's thought into judgment over our sickness and disease.

This is the kind of action the Scriptures demand from you and me. First of all, we must see that God's Word works. Secondly, we must determine to *do* it— to *walk it out.* We accomplish this by making the Word become the judge over all the thoughts of the devil. Praise God! When this happens in your life, you will be set free. The key is found in learning how to *do* the Word of God.

4

The Key to Great Faith

The concepts we've discussed thus far, concerning the battle we have with our thoughts and the importance of the Word of God, are foundational to the direct theme of this book: "How does praise release powerful faith?"

Praise must relate directly to the Word of God. Praise must use the Word as a weapon. Praise is the launching vehicle; the Word contains the power. ***Praise releases faith when it launches the Word of God.***

Let's now take a closer look at how to release the power of our faith through the action of praise. "By him therefore let us offer the sacrifice of praise to God continually, that is, the fruit of our lips giving thanks to his name" (Heb. 13:15). This is the classic verse on praise in the New Testament especially as it relates to the sacrifice of praise.

Let us note several preliminary points concerning this verse before we examine it in depth. The writer to the Hebrews is instructing each one of us in the Church to offer a sacrifice of praise to God continually. This means all the time: every day the praise of God is to be on our lips. It is to be a sacrifice of praise, and we will discuss the important connection between sacrifice and praise later in this chapter.

Praise is to be "the fruit of our lips." That means it must be verbal. It must be spoken, articulated aloud. The mouth has to be used in the act of praise. (Remember, God is after our mouths in the same way the devil is after our mouths).

The final phrase in Hebrews 13:15 is "...giving thanks to his name."The sacrifice of praise is, therefore, giving thanks (or as a marginal translations says, "confessing to His name").

The Principle of Sacrifice

A close examination of Scripture reveals that the principle of sacrifice is found everywhere in the Scriptures. It was first established in the Old Testament as a result of the original sin of Adam and Eve. God has always required a sacrifice of mankind. When He called for a sacrifice, He asked the people to bring the very best of their substance and to present it in a very specific manner to Him as an offering. This principle is at the heart of every act of sacrifice. God demanded the shedding of innocent blood for the covering of man's sin.

Since those early times, God's laws have not changed. When Christ died on the cross for our sins 2,000 years ago, He satisfied God's justice. Innocent blood was shed for the covering of man's sin. Christ's death did not abolish the need for sacrifice in our lives.

The New Testament illustrates this principle again in Hebrews 13:15: "...let us offer the sacrifice of praise to God continually." In 2 Samuel 24 and 1 Chronicles 21, we have excellent examples of the meaning of sacrifice. David had sinned in numbering the people of Israel. The wrath of God was kindled against him and the Lord sent a pestilence upon Israel. A death angel began to stretch his hand over Jerusalem to destroy it. David immediately repented before the Lord and in return God commanded David to offer sacrifices in a special way and in a special place.

The Lord told him to build an altar on the threshing floor of Ornan the Jubusite. It was during the time of the harvest. Ornan, of course, was a farmer. To shut down his threshing floor to build an altar would be to shut down the source of his income at the most important time of the year.

The Bible says that Ornan also saw the death angel hovering over the city of Jerusalem. Immediately he offered his threshing floor to David at no cost. He begged David to take the threshing floor and even offered his own oxen to be used as burnt offerings and his threshing implements to be used for the wood of sacrifice. Ornan was offering to David everything God had commanded of David.

At this point David faced a great temptation. ***Would he offer to God the free gifts Ornan had offered to him?*** David knew in his heart, that if he did this, he would miss the entire idea of sacrifice. God had demanded a sacrifice of David, not of Ornan, but Ornan's offer constituted a temptation for David nonetheless. It could have become the easy way out. Down in his heart, however, David knew that the key of sacrifice involved himself. He had to make the sacrifice. He realized it would be an insult to the character of God to offer sacrifices that cost him nothing. So David refused the sacrifice of Ornan with these words: "...Nay; but I will surely buy it of thee at a price: neither will I offer burnt offerings unto the Lord my God of that which doth cost me nothing." The verse continues, "So David bought the threshingfloor and the oxen for fifty shekels of silver" (2 Sam. 24:24).

The Offer of Ornan

The message of this story is that sacrifice must touch our lives; it must cost us something. The "offer of Ornan" is being made to people in churches across the land every Sunday morning. it is so easy to slip into the back of the church, sit down and listen to the sacrifices offered by the choir, the music director and the pastor. It is so easy to accept their sacrifices on our behalf. The choir may sing beautifully, the pastor may have an excellent message, and we come with a desire to be ministered to. But in accepting "the offer of Ornan," we miss the essence of sacrifice.

Hebrews 13:15 says, "...let us offer the sacrifice of praise to God continually." This means we are to do so in every part of our day and it means especially that we should do so when we come to the house of the Lord. God asks His people to offer a sacrifice of praise to Him. It must touch us intimately; it must come from the depths of our hearts. *Only when it costs something does it become a sacrifice.*

I have stood in the midst of praise services in some of the largest churches of this nation and others. I have watched people go through the ritual of a perfunctory form of praise. Many have become professionals at it. They raise their hands to the right height; they intone the words with the proper inflection of voice. But it is obvious from the expressions on their faces that they are preoccupied with affairs of business, an argument on the way to church, the clothes that someone else is wearing in the service, or in watching what the choir is doing on the platform. The point is that there is no sacrifice involved in their praise.

I know many charismatic people who can praise God with their minds on "auto-pilot." There is just as much ritual in their praise as there is in the main-line denominations from which they have come. Romans 8:7 says, "...the carnal mind is enmity against God: for it is not subject to the law of God, neither indeed can be." *The carnal mind does not want to enter into praise and worship.* The devil will do everything he can to manipulate our thoughts so as to prevent us from participation in praise and worship. He will cause us to think about the children, about the roast in the oven at home— anything that prevents us from having our minds dwelling on the majesty and glory of God.

There is a tremendous battle in every worship service at this point. The mind wants to rule us. The mind wants to control us. The mind does not want to submit itself to the flow of the Spirit in the action of praise and worship. That's why praise is a powerful tool of God for the renewing of the mind. The enemy brings thoughts, suggestions, anything he can, to divert our minds from meditating on the majesty and glory of God. He knows if he does this, he will destroy the power resulting from praise in the church.

Speaking To Our Minds

Notice how David approached the subject of praise. He says: "Bless the Lord, O my soul: and all that is within me, bless his holy name" (Ps. 103:1). David is talking to his soul; he is talking to his mind. He is commanding his mind to bless the Lord. Sometimes we have to do that. We have to grab the attention of our minds and say, *"Mind, praise the Lord!* I don't care what else you want to think about, I don't care where you want to focus your attention. Right now you're going to focus your attention on the Lord. Mind, you're going to bless the Lord."

Notice how David gets his mind focused on the glory of God. He says, "...forget not all of his benefits" (Ps. 103:2). Meditate on the blessings of God. Meditate on the fact that your sins have been forgiven. Meditate on the One who heals all your diseases. Remember the times when God has touched you in your body and healed those in your family. This is how to get your mind to bless the Lord. This is what the sacrifice of praise is all about.

But it is much easier for the average believer to accept the offer of Ornan. It's easy to sit and listen to a radio program or a television program and enjoy the sacrifices offered by the speaker and the musicians. It's another thing entirely to enter into the action of the sacrifice of praise on a regular and daily basis. This is God's demand of every believer.

The Sacrifice of Praise

Sacrifice also involves several other aspects. God is not interested only in the praise we give Him when things are going well. He is after that praise that comes in the midst of great trial, great difficulty, grief, sickness, demonic oppression, temptation, relational difficulties and financial problems. He still requires praise. He still demands it. When we give it to Him in our times of difficulty, it means all the more to Him.

We become like Paul and Silas in the Philippian jail, praising God at midnight, even though they hurt so badly. We become like Jonah in the belly of the great fish, as he prayed and said, "...I will sacrifice unto thee with the voice of thanksgiving" (Jonah 2:9). It's hard to thank God when you're in the belly of a fish. That involves sacrifice. But there is something about the costliness of the sacrifice that touches the heart of God. It was the act of sacrifice that brought the shaking of the prison for Paul and Silas. It was the act of sacrifice that made that big fish deposit Jonah on dry ground. *There is a spiritual hot-button in the action of the sacrifice of praise.* It moves us into miracles. It moves us into the divine action of Almighty God.

I had to learn this personally in the midst of great tragedy. When my late wife was killed instantly, I was plunged into the midst of deep grief. I had to praise the Lord aloud, when everything inside of me was shattered. The devil fought me every step of the way. He called me a hypocrite for praising the Lord when I felt so badly. But I had to learn the lesson of sacrifice. When I did, God led me into the ministry of praise and healing.

Let us examine now the second phrase of Hebrews 13:15: "...the fruit of our lips giving thanks to his name." In my King James Bible, there is a marginal note for the phrase, "giving thanks." The literal translation of this phrase is: "confessing to His name." This is verified in the American Standard Version and the Berkley Version which translate the phrase as: "lips that make confession to His name." A close examination of the original Greek indicates that the word translated "giving thanks" has been translated from the original Greek word *homologeo*. In most other places in the New Testament *homologeo* is translated "to confess."

The latter part of Hebrews 13:15, therefore, should be correctly translated, "That is, the fruit of lips confessing to His name." This is one of the most powerful revelations God has ever given me in the praise and worship message. The writer of Hebrews 13:15 is telling us that we are to offer a sacrifice of praise to God continually. The words "that is" tell us of what the sacrifice of praise consists. **The sacrifice of praise, therefore, is equated with confession to the Name of Jesus.** They are the same thing.

Let us examine the word *homologeo* more thoroughly. In the *Expository Dictionary of New Testament Words* by W. E. Vine, *homologeo* is defined as "to confess." Literally, it means "to speak the same thing, to give assent to, to agree with, to confess, to declare, to confess by way of admitting one's guilt, to confess or declare openly by way of speaking out freely (such confession being the effect of deep conviction of faith), *to confess by way of celebrating with praise.*"

Confession in Praise

We have here a revelation of the connection between New Testament confession and the sacrifice of praise. It is absolutely necessary for every Christian to understand the place confession holds in the teaching of the New Testament. Almost invariably when the word confession is used, most people think of confessing their sins and transgressions. Confession does mean that, but that is the negative connotation of the word. On the positive side, it means the confession of our faith in God's Word. Homologeo—to confess, means "saying the same as." In other words, confession is saying the same thing with our mouth that God says in His Word. It is literally making the words of our mouth agree with the written Word of God.

Romans 10:10 says, "For with the heart man believeth unto righteousness; and with the mouth confession is made unto salvation." We must confess our way into the benefits of salvation. If faith is going to move in our lives, it must have a means of expressing itself. The words of our lips give expression and life to the action of faith within us. Faith, to be real faith, has to speak. It has to express itself. If it does not speak, it is stillborn.

This is so true of the sacrifice of praise. That is why real praise must be spoken; it must be expressed. The mouth must be used. It is the action of sacrifice that explodes us into the area of faith and this then begins to prepare us for the mighty miracles of God.

It becomes readily evident in the New Testament that **there is a direct connection between our mouths and our hearts.** The Bible says, "...for out of the abundance of the heart the mouth speaketh" (Matt. 12:34). If we have something in our hearts, it will invariably find a way of expressing itself through our mouths. You can't separate the one from the other. The mouth is like a faucet that lets out whatever is being held inside the heart. If our heart is filled with the Word of God, if we are standing in faith on what God's Word says, then that faith will be expressed out of our mouth.

On the other hand, if we are filled with unbelief and fear, if we are bound by the strongholds of thought Satan has established in our lives, that condition will manifest itself by coming forth out of our mouths. That is how Satan attacks the average believer. He manipulates our thoughts; he whispers in our minds and says, "You have all the symptoms of a tumor in the brain." He wants those evil thoughts to capture our hearts. He wants fear to grip us. He wants our minds meditating on those thoughts so they can find their way inside of us. The more we meditate on thoughts like these, the more they take control of our hearts.

The ultimate plan of the devil, however, is to gain control of our mouths. He wants us to speak the fear that is in our hearts. As I said before, the mouth is the center of spiritual warfare for the universe. Once the heart is captured, Satan knows that our mouths will speak out of the abundance of our hearts; then, when he has control of the mouth, he has control of the believer. He is able to throw his rockets of gossip, backbiting, division, hatred, fear, lies, and so on. When he has control of our mouths, then he has control of us. That is how disease oftentimes captures a believer.

Mouth and Heart

Romans 10:8-10 deals with the subject of confession. Notice the way the two words, "mouth" and "heart" appear in these verses.

> **8 But what sayeth it? The word is nigh thee, even in thy *mouth,* and in thy *heart:* that is, the word of faith, which we preach;**
> **9 That if thou shalt confess with thy *mouth* the**

Lord Jesus, and shalt believe in thine *heart* that God
hath raised him from the dead, thou shalt be saved.
10 For with the *heart* man believeth unto righteousness; and with the *mouth* confession is made unto salvation.

In verse 8 Paul mentions the mouth first and the
heart second. In verse 9 it is the mouth first and the
heart second. But in verse 10 the order is reversed
and the heart is mentioned first and the mouth second.

This illustrates a very important Scriptural principle. **You must say God's Word with your mouth
until you get it in your heart.** When we come to the
Word of God and apply it against an attack of the
devil, we move into spiritual warfare. For example, if
we are sick in our bodies, we need to begin to declare
a verse that speaks of God's healing. The principle of
the use of mouth and heart in these three verses in
Romans shows us that it is necessary for us to come
against the disease by putting God's Word in our
mouths. It is an act of our wills. We bring the Word
against the sickness by confessing it or saying the
same thing with our mouth as God says in His Word.

When we do this we begin to receive it into our
heart. The more often we confess with our mouth, the
more firmly it becomes established in our heart.
There comes a time when the heart responds to what
the mouth has been saying. The heart begins to believe the confession of the mouth. There is a moment
of *rhema* revelation and the heart believes what the
mouth is saying. Then the order is reversed. The
mouth then naturally expresses what the heart believes. This process is necessary for the reeducation of
the heart. The confession of what God's Word says is
necessary to reeducate our minds. In the Hebrew language the phrase, "to learn by heart" actually is
translated "to learn by mouth." That is how we learn
the best.

I remember some of the poems I had to learn in grade school, "Mary had a Little Lamb" and others. I repeated them over and over again with my mouth until I knew them in my heart. It is the same with the process of confession. What is seven times seven? Forty-nine. How do you know that? You know that because when you were a child, you said the multiplication tables over and over until they became a part of the understanding of your heart.

This is what happens with the Word of God. Every time we are attacked by the devil, we come to God's Word and we begin to confess it. Obviously, this involves a struggle. The Word of God is saying something contrary to what we are experiencing. Our feelings will tell us that the Word of God is not true. But the very process of confession demands that we resist our feelings and make the words of our mouth agree with God's Word. Sooner or later the struggle will be over and then it becomes a natural process for us to speak with our mouth exactly what God says in His Word.

Don't Give Up

My wife, Shirley, has one of the most powerful testimonies I have heard in this area. Shirley and her husband Jim had been happily married for eleven years. One day Jim experienced a seizure and was taken to the hospital. Shirley fainted when the doctor told her that Jim had an inoperable tumor in the brain. They didn't know how much longer he would live.

It was two and a half years before Jim passed away. Gradually he began to lose the ability to work and earn a living. Shirley was forced to take a job to support herself, Jim and their two children. Jim had been a successful stockbroker with a good salary. Her salary was much lower than his and their family began to suffer.

It became very difficult to pay the regular bills on the house, gas, electric, telephone, let alone buy food for the family. Many nights their children, Jason and Marie, went to bed with cold cereal for supper. Shirley had to work all day, prepare meals when she got home, cut the lawn, nurse Jim, and care for the children. There was no money to fix appliances when they malfunctioned. The washing machine broke down, the oven hadn't worked for three months, then the car broke down as well.

Shirley had two choices—she could give up or fight. She chose to fight. She realized she was under a direct attack from Satan. She also realized that her weapon was the Word of God. She wrote down Scripture verses. She taped them on the mirror in the bathroom. She tacked them on the visor in the car. Everywhere she went she would quote the Scriptures and stand on the Word of God. She was saying them with her mouth until she got them down into her heart. She would say, "The joy of the Lord is my strength," when to all appearances there was no joy in her life. She did this faithfully for a year and a half and nothing seemed to change.

One day on her way to work, in the company car, it was like the devil sat beside her in the passenger seat. He said, "A lot of good it does you to trust the Lord and quote Scripture. Look at you. Your husband is dying, your appliances are broken down. You don't have food in your house. Christmas is coming and you can't buy gifts for your children. You are fooling yourself."

Shirley made a decision. She stopped the car and began to quote the Word of God to the devil. Then she got out of the car, on the side of the freeway, and she ran around the car with her hands in the air praising the Lord for the fact that "His joy was her strength," that "He was meeting her financial needs according to His riches in glory." When she got back in the car she knew she had won a victory.

That night her neighbor called her. Her neighbor was not a professing believer. She was crying. She said, "Shirley, I can't buy meat for my family until I buy some for you. Do you need any?" She had no idea of their financial situation. She filled their freezer full of meat.

A short time later, while Shirley was out ministering to a family in their church, a man stopped by the house. He told a strange story. He had been on his way to the mall close by when he had a vision of Shirley and Jim's house. The Lord told him to stop and give them $200 cash. The children had Christmas presents that year. Time and time again the Lord met their needs in miraculous ways. Shirley said she came into a "knowing" that God would honor His Word in her life. She said it with her mouth until she believed it in her heart.

Hebrews 13:15 declares that the sacrifice of praise is the fruit of lips that make confession to His Name. The sacrifice of praise must be made in the face of extreme obstacles, in the midst of satanic attack. When we praise God, using the Word; using a special verse in the Word that relates to our situation, we praise ourselves into healing. We praise ourselves into the many benefits of God. Praise in this context becomes an act of the will rather than an act of the feelings.

The sacrifice of praise literally involves confession to the Name of Jesus. Feelings cannot dictate to us. Feelings fluctuate and will move us away from the truth of the Word. But when we stand with that sacrifice of praise, we prepare ourselves for a mighty miracle from God. In Romans 10:10 Paul says, "For with the heart man believeth unto righteousness; and with the mouth confession is made unto salvation."

The next chapter will show that the confession of

righteousness is the foundation for the sacrifice of praise. You have to know that you have been made righteous before you can begin to confess or flow in the sacrifice of praise. The last part of Romans 10:10 says, "...and with the mouth confession is made unto salvation." The word "unto" indicates a motion or progress. In other words, we move progressively into the various elements of our salvation, as we continue to make the right confession with our mouths.

It is necessary to understand the New Testament meaning of the word "salvation" in order to understand the overwhelming power of confession in the mouth of the believer. This will be discussed at length in a future chapter. Because confession and the sacrifice of praise are the same thing, this will shed brand new light on the power of praise and worship in the heart of the believer.

Key to Faith

Confession is the key to our faith. It is the key that unlocks the wealth of God's promises on our behalf. This is an incredible truth that every believer must appropriate. We take hold of God's provision for us in every area of our lives by entering into a confession or a sacrifice of praise. That is why I believe that the sacrifice of praise and worship will lead us into a total manifestation of the entire salvation provided for us on the cross by Jesus Christ.

Let me repeat this important truth: **the sacrifice of praise essentially is an act of confession to the Word, the Name, and the Blood.** The sacrifice of praise is saying the same thing with our lips that God says in His Word. The sacrifice of praise is taking the words of the Psalms, the promises of the New Testament, and singing them, raising them as a triumphant anthem in the presence of God. By doing this we move our feelings and the symptoms of our bodies into line with the declared Word of God and we begin to see a manifestation of the healing power of the Lord.

When I first received a command from the Lord to lead people into His presence for the healing of the sick, I did not understand how healing was connected with praise and worship. I began to do exactly as the Lord said by holding meetings where I would lead people into the presence of the Lord through praise and worship. I noticed a tremendous flow of healing power moving through the services. I didn't know why it happened, I just knew that it worked. It was only as God began to open this particular verse in Hebrews 13:15 to my heart, that I began to understand the tremendous key this verse contained.

In leading an entire congregation into a corporate sacrifice of praise, if they will push all extraneous thoughts out of their minds; if they will begin to focus on the awesome majesty and power of Almighty God; if their hearts will come into unity by uplifting the power of the Name of Jesus, then we are able to experience mass corporate confession.

An entire congregation moves thereby into a faith declaration. Their mouths have come under the Lordship of Jesus Christ. It is the sacrifice of praise that releases them into a flow of divine healing energy. This healing energy moves against the power of thoughts and strongholds that have bound the lives and bodies of men and women in my meetings. Numerous healings become the evidence of the confession of God's children. It is impossible for me to overemphasize the power of the principle I have just expressed.

The Lord impressed me several years ago to take praise and healing to the Roman Catholic churches of Poland. He told me if I would teach them the Sacrifice of Praise, He would heal the sick. At first I was afraid to do it. "It is hard to communicate this truth across language barriers," I told myself. But I determined to be obedient.

I would preach a simple gospel message in the crusades, pray the sinner's prayer with the people, and then lead them into praise and worship. I remember my first prayer for the sick. When I asked every one who had been healed to raise their hands, I was sure no one would raise their hands. You can imagine my surprise and joy when two blind eyes were opened and a goiter the size of half an apple disappeared from a 13-year-old girl's throat. The audience was electrified. That night we could not seat the people in the building—many were out on the street.

Any pastor can lead his people into an act of corporate confession through the sacrifice of praise. He can teach them the principles of bringing their minds into subjection to the mind of Christ. That entire audience can focus their attention on the glory of God. They can raise their voices in an anthem of praise. If they do, there will be a release of power and energy in their services that will bring healing to the sick, that will tear down strongholds, and that will manifest the power of God. *That is how praise releases powerful faith.*

The High Priesthood of Jesus

Now let us look at it from another perspective. What happens on God's side in heaven when we move into the sacrifice of praise down here? How does Jesus respond? How does our heavenly Father respond to the praise of His people? The high priesthood of Jesus Christ reveals the answers to us.

In the book of Hebrews we have a main theme which accents the high priesthood of Jesus Christ. It really is a revelation of the ministry Jesus has at the right hand of the Father on our behalf. That means Jesus is seated at the right hand of the Father for us. He ministers as our personal representative in the presence of God. He presents our prayer requests and praise. Finally He becomes a surety or a guarantee for the fulfillment of God's promises on our behalf. These are tremendously important points that demand our attention, even our meditation.

A high priest in Old Testament times was someone who went into the presence of God on behalf of others. On the Day of Atonement, the high priest would take the blood of the lamb into the Holy of Holies. He would place it on the Mercy Seat before God in the presence of the Shekinah Glory. That blood would become a covering for the sins of the nation. Let me emphasize that the high priest represented the people in the presence of God. In the same way, Jesus Christ has gone unto the Father as our High Priest. He represents us to the Father and in representing us, He brings our requests, our prayers, our praise, to the Father.

A close reading of the book of Hebrews reveals something else concerning the high priesthood of Jesus. The high priesthood of Jesus Christ on our behalf is directly linked to the confession of our mouths. In other words, the confession we make here on earth determines how much Jesus is able to minister on our behalf in heaven. ***He only goes as far as our confession permits Him.***

Confession and Our High Priest

Let's examine the Scripture. In Hebrews 3:1 we are exhorted to consider Jesus Christ as the High Priest of our confession. This links Christ's high priesthood directly to our confession. It is our confession that makes His priestly ministry effective on our behalf. He will only bring our confession of the Word to the Father. He will not bring our begging and our crying and our pleading. Only when we stand on God's Word and declare it true concerning ourselves, will our High Priest bring that declaration to the Father.

Each time we make the right confession, we have the authority of Christ as our High Priest behind us. He becomes a guarantee of that which we confess. If we confess doubt or unbelief, then Christ has no opportunity to minister as our High Priest. You see, our mouths are the key. When we launch our weapons with our mouths, our High Priest goes into action at the right hand of the Father on our behalf. ***Right confession invokes His high priestly ministry, but wrong confession shuts us off from it.***

That is why it is so unwise for a believer to say in a church service, "I will not praise God; I will not open my mouth and raise my voice in praise unto the Lord. I don't feel like it. I will not be manipulated, so consequently I will not praise." What does a person do when he makes that kind of statement? He shuts himself off from the blessings of God. He shuts himself off from the high priesthood of Jesus Christ. The High Priest cannot take his confession to the Father. This is absolutely awesome in its implications.

Let's look further. In Hebrews 4:14, the writer again links the high priesthood of Jesus directly to our confession. "Seeing then that we have a great high priest, that is passed into the heavens, Jesus the Son of God, let us hold fast our profession [confession]." The emphasis here is on holding fast so that Jesus will be able to continue with His High Priestly ministry on our behalf.

It is evident when we make our words line up with the Word of God, when we bring those words against the symptoms and disease in our bodies, there is going be to conflict. The devil will bombard our minds with thoughts. He will try to get us under the load of the disease. But this verse encourages us to hold fast our confession. We are to hold fast in the face of satanic onslaught.

Once we have brought the words of our mouths into agreement with God's written Word, we must be careful not to change or go back to a position of unbelief. Many pressures will come against us. It will seem that everything is contrary to us but we stand with our confession. We continue to hold on to the Word of God.

The next passage we want to look at is Hebrews 10:21 and 23. Here the writer of the epistle is, for the third time, stressing the connection between Christ's priesthood and our confession.

21 And having an high priest over the house of God;
23 Let us hold fast the profession [confession] of our faith without wavering..."

Notice that in the three passages of Hebrews under present consideration there is mounting emphasis on the importance of maintaining a right confession. In Hebrews 3:1 we are told that Jesus is the High Priest of our confession. In Hebrews 4:14 we are exhorted to hold fast to our confession. In Hebrews 10:23 we are exhorted to hold fast to our confession without wavering. The suggestion here is that we are likely to be subjected to ever-increasing pressures that would change or weaken our confession.

You'll Be Tested

Let me illustrate this truth with a personal story. In 1978 I went into the Soviet Union with Living Sound for the first time. The Lord gave me an opportunity to meet one of the leaders of the underground church. One night this leader said to me, "Terry, we need a printing press to print the Word of God here in the Soviet Union. Can you get it for us?" I told him I would pray about it and after praying for a short time, I sensed a witness of the Spirit. I told him, "Yes, I will do it."

When I left the Soviet Union, I flew into London, England, for a boardmeeting with some of our men there. About 3:00 one morning as I knelt by my bed in prayer, I asked the Lord, "How will I ever be able to pay for a printing press?" The Lord spoke to my spirit, "There will be someone in your board meeting in Tulsa in two weeks who will have the money for the press." This impression was so strong within my spirit that I knew I had heard from the Lord.

Two weeks later we had an American and Canadian board meeting in Tulsa. Over forty men came from various cities. One night we had a banquet which included our Tulsa supporters. I stood up in the meeting and said, "God has told me that there is someone here to whom He has spoken concerning a gift of $15,000 for the purchase of a printing press."

There were about 600 people in the room when I made the announcement. I had no question that someone would respond immediately. I stood on the platform waiting. A minute, two minutes went by, but it appeared that no one was willing to stand. As three minutes passed, I was getting embarrassed. By the time three and a half minutes had come and gone, I began to fear. I quickly moved on to another part of the program.

On the inside I was shattered. *I had embarrassed myself in front of 600 people.* I had looked like a fool to them and to myself. I went home that night humiliated. I knelt by my bed and said, "Lord, I can never face those men in the board meeting tomorrow morning. They have lost all respect for me. I said that I heard your voice when obviously I did not."

In spite of this, I went back the next morning. One of the men stood up and said, "Terry, you should not have made a statement like that unless you were certain God had spoken to you." I stood there with a tremendous struggle going on inside. Finally, I said to the men, "I don't understand it but I know that God has spoken to someone about that $15,000 and obviously that person was not obedient."

As soon as I said those words, one of the brothers stood up. He had been brought to our board meeting as a guest from Canada. He told us that two weeks earlier God had spoken to him about bringing $15,000 to the board meeting. He thought it was his own mind playing tricks on him so he didn't do it. He was a new convert in Christ and had only received Jesus about six months previously. When I mentioned the $15,000 figure he was so startled that he was afraid to respond. But now in this meeting he told the men he would honor that commitment by providing the $15,000. He followed through, and subsequently, that press was delivered.

The point I am trying to make with this story is that I was subjected to tremendous pressure concerning my confession. The devil came at me with every negative thought you can imagine to try to turn me from the declaration of what God had spoken in my spirit. If I had turned from my confession that man would never have stood and admitted what God had spoken in his heart. But because I stayed with the confession, and stayed with the revelation God had given to me, the miracle did come forth. That's why in Hebrews 10:23 the writer says, "Let us hold fast the profession [confession] of our faith without wavering." That is how miracles come.

Hold Fast

By way of review, please permit me to stress again the importance of the connection between the sacrifice of praise and the confession of the believer. Hebrews 13:15 says we are to offer up that sacrifice of praise to God continually. We are to do it every day. We are to **hold fast** to that confession of the sacrifice of praise.

This indicates the tremendous potential of praise in the life of the believer. ***Your praise literally releases Jesus at the right hand of the Father to operate on your behalf.*** If we make the wrong confession, He has no opportunity to minister as our High Priest. If we refuse to enter into praise, we refuse to allow Jesus to help us.

That is why the devil attacks us in the midst of a praise service. The devil does not want you to enter into the wonderful things God has for you. The devil wants your thoughts manipulated and focused on anything other than the glory of God. If he can do that, then he will rob you and rob the church of the miracle-working power of God. The devil knows that as soon a you enter into praise you will begin to confess the Word of God in your praise. You will use the Word as the weapon God meant it to be. As your praise and worship uses the Word, it will begin to smash the strongholds of disease and bondage the devil has put on you. Therefore, the devil is committed to stopping your praise because in doing that he is stopping your confession.

Can you see how important it is to stand in the midst of praise in the same way you stand with the confession of your faith? The two are synonymous. When we stand in the sacrifice of praise, immediately our High Priest, Jesus Christ, goes to work at the right hand of the Father on our behalf. He offers our praise to the Father as our personal representative.

When I stand before an audience and lead 1,000 people into the presence of God with a sacrifice of praise, the High Priest of that sacrifice takes the confession of that congregation and brings it, in a corporate sense, to the Father. He says, "Father, here is what my children are saying, here is the praise they are offering. It is a sweet-smelling fragrance in our nostrils. Father, ***honor the faith expressed by that*** *praise."* Then we begin to see miracles. We begin to see people being set free by the almighty power of God. I am absolutely convinced that if you can see the truth of what I am saying here, you will move yourself into an area of faith unlike any you've known before. *This is precisely how praise releases powerful faith.*

5

Righteousness is the Foundation

A Heart Established In Righteousness

In the previous chapter we developed the theme of the sacrifice of praise and related it directly to the confession of the believer. We showed how the sacrifice of praise is confession to the Name of Jesus. Therefore, the principles that make confession work also make the sacrifice of praise work. If the sacrifice of praise is the confession of the believer, then simple logic dictates that the laws of confession relate directly to the sacrifice of praise. Whatever makes confession work will make the sacrifice of praise work.

As we've already pointed out, Romans 10:10 is a very important verse regarding the action of confession in the believer's life. That verse says, "For with the heart man believeth unto righteousness; and with the mouth confession is made unto salvation." We could restate the verse simply as follows, "It is necessary for a man to believe in righteousness with his heart before his mouth makes confession to the action of salvation."

In other words, before we begin to confess with our mouths and to expect the miracle-working power of God, we must first have a heart that is established in righteousness. This means we will never really come into the true power of the sacrifice of praise until we have first understood the concept of Biblical righteousness.

Righteousness is like a foundation that gives power to our confession. It gives power to the sacrifice of praise. Therefore, it is absolutely essential for us to examine the operation of righteousness in the life of the believer. Paul says, "For with the heart man believeth unto righteousness..." We have to get the concept and the truth of righteousness into our hearts. When this is done, then with great confidence we can begin to make our confession. With great confidence we can enter into the sacrifice of praise.

Many Christians, however, have not understood this truth. They have launched themselves into the action of confession with disastrous results. There are many people today who have seen the truth of confession in the Scriptures and have begun to practice it regularly in their lives, but they have never seen the truth of righteousness. Consequently, the action of confession has not produced fruit.

There is one primary reason for the failure of this kind of confession. The believer has not seen that righteousness is connected to the action of confession. *Unless your praise is founded on an overwhelming sense of righteousness, it cannot be true praise.* It degenerates into ritual, into liturgical form. It loses its power and life. You can truly enter into the sacrifice of praise when you fully understand the concept of your righteousness in Christ.

In this chapter, therefore, we will examine the subject of the righteousness of the believer. As we study this and allow the truth of God's Word to penetrate our beings, we will find ourselves in a position of strong faith. We will be prepared for entrance into the sacrifice of praise.

Righteousness is the Key Theme of the Bible

Righteousness is a key theme of the Bible. It is the central message of the Old and New Testaments. In the Old Testament, God gave man the Law in order to demonstrate His divine righteousness. It was also patently obvious that by the deeds of the Law, no man could fully satisfy the righteousness of God.

The New Testament is God's answer to the problem of righteousness. Jesus Christ became the door. As we trust in Him, God grants us complete righteousness. That means one-hundred-percent righteousness. There is no such thing as being partially righteous.

Perhaps you feel that because you prayed a little longer in your devotions today, or read an extra chapter from the Scriptures, or perhaps witnessed to someone about your faith, that you are a little closer to God. Becoming more faithful in our devotional activities does not make us more righteous.

Righteousness is not predicated on man's works. We are either one-hundred-percent righteous or we are not righteous at all. That is fundamental. God does not grade on a curve. You either have it or you don't have it.

There is only one word in both Hebrew and Greek that translates the two terms *"just"* and *"righteous."* "Just" is understood more as a legal term, a term of the courts, whereas "righteous" is related more to the way we live in a practical sense. But this distinction is not found in the Scriptures. There is no difference between the meanings of being justified or being made righteous. This means that a man who truly understands that he has been made righteous by faith in God is going to work out that righteousness by godly actions.

The King James Version uses the term "justified" many times in the New Testament. It is a good Scriptural discipline to interchange the term "made righteous" every time you read the term "justified." This will bring home the strong accent Paul places on righteousness in the book of Romans.

The Gospel Declares Righteousness

Have you ever noticed what Paul says in Romans 1:16? "...I am not ashamed of the gospel of Christ: for it is the power of God unto salvation to every one that believeth..." Then in the next verse he reveals the core of the power in the gospel. He says, "For therein is the righteousness of God revealed from faith to faith, as it is written, the just [righteous] shall live by faith" (italics mine). Paul is giving us here an explosive insight into the essence of the gospel. The reason the gospel has power is because the gospel is a declaration of righteousness.

It is the job of the preachers of the land to declare to the people that they can be righteous if they will trust Christ. It is the job of every preacher to make people feel righteous, not to make them feel guilty. We must make them realize righteousness.

It is only as a man sees his righteousness that he is able, by faith, to move into the blessings of God. It is only by being aware of his righteousness that a man is able to enter into the sacrifice of praise and experience the miracles God has for him.

Years ago in my preaching I used to feel it was my job to make people feel guilty. I would call them to the altar and many would kneel there weeping. I thought I was putting them under the conviction of the Holy Spirit. There are times obviously when the Holy Spirit will convict a man of sin. However, when a believer is trusting Christ, it then becomes our job to get his mind off the sin, and onto the righteousness imputed to him in Christ. If he can see his righteousness in Christ, he won't be looking at his sin, and consequently won't be falling into sin all the time.

Rather, he will be establishing himself in the power of God released through the sense of his own righteousness. "...seek ye first the kingdom of God, and his righteousness and all these things [the blessings of God] shall be added unto you" (Matthew 6:33).

Receiving From God

Let us examine Romans 4:4, "Now to him that worketh is the reward not reckoned of grace, but of debt." The teaching of this verse is fundamental. Wages are something you earn. In other words, if God blesses us and we think we have earned it, then we feel He has blessed us because of our good deeds. Somehow we think God becomes indebted to us, that God has to bless us because of what we have done. This is wrong thinking.

So many believers have difficulty receiving anything from God. In fact, I think we need to teach a class in our churches on how God's people can learn to receive God's gifts. This is a great problem. It is difficult for people to receive healing, to receive financial blessings. We simply can't receive because we feel that God only rewards our own righteousness. Everything in life teaches us that we have to work in order to earn. So many people cannot get healed because of this very problem.

Verse 5 says, "But to him that worketh not, but believeth on him that justifieth [makes righteous] the ungodly, his faith is counted for righteousness." Notice the first phrase in that verse, "...to him that worketh not." That is the key. **Relax. Take it easy. It's a free gift.** In receiving, you simply have to stop trying and receive. If any part of you continues trying to earn, God won't do it because it's not of grace.

Stop striving and struggling and begging and take a position of righteousness. The principle is so simple: you cannot earn God's grace. Grace, by the very meaning of the word, means "God's unmerited favor." There is no way you can buy it; it's a gift of God.

Justification by Faith

How often has it happened that the old saint who has been living the Christian life for thirty years is not healed even though he has reminded God of his good deeds? So many times I have seen an alcoholic or a prostitute come walking into a service, become born again and get healed and blessed of God instantaneously. The old saint might stand back and say, "But it's not fair." That person simply hasn't understood. God doesn't heal because of good works. God heals because we trust and believe in His grace. In fact, God can't heal until we stop trying to earn.

In Romans 10, Paul is upset about his people, the children of Israel. They have lived for fifteen centuries with one uppermost problem. In verse 3 Paul describes it as follows, "For they being ignorant of God's righteousness, and going about to establish their own righteousness, have not submitted themselves unto the righteousness of God." That says it better than any verse in the entire Bible: "...they being ignorant of God's righteousness."

How many believers today are ignorant concerning God's righteousness? It is so hard for a believer not to depend upon his own good works. Every one of us wants to go about establishing our own righteousness but in doing that we don't submit ourselves to the righteousness of God. Therefore, we do not receive our healing. He cannot move us into the blessings the way He would like to. It takes humility to say, "I am made righteous by faith." It takes humility to bow before God and to receive His gift of righteousness. But what blessings come with that act of humility!

Here's the Key

Now we come to the great text in Romans 10:8-10 (italics are mine):

> **8 But what saith it? The word is nigh thee, even in thy *mouth,* and in thy *heart:* that is, the word of faith, which we preach;**
>
> **9 That if thou shalt confess with thy *mouth* the Lord Jesus, and shalt believe in thine *heart* that God hath raised him from the dead, thou shalt be saved.**
>
> **10 For with the *heart* man believeth unto righteousness; and with the *mouth* confession is made unto salvation.**

In an earlier chapter I asked you to notice the words *"mouth"* and *"heart"* in this text. In verse 8, mouth comes before heart; in verse 9, mouth precedes heart as well; but in verse 10, the heart comes before the mouth. This is a divine example of how we grow in faith. We put God's Word in our mouths and its truth comes into our hearts as we say it with our mouths. We must continue to repeat it and confess it with our mouths so that our hearts will believe it. Then our hearts grasp what our mouths have been saying and our mouths can confess their way into the many blessings of salvation God provides.

We get the blessing of God by believing in our hearts and saying with our mouths. And that, my friend, is precisely how you receive the reality of the gift of righteousness.

This is the great key I want you to see. You receive the truth of righteousness by declaring it with your mouth until you start to believe it in your heart. You must say it over and over again with your mouth until sooner or later your heart picks it up. When your heart picks it up you will catch the *rhema* revelation of righteousness.

Based on that tremendous foundation, you can

move yourself into the blessings of God. You can praise your way into all of the blessings of salvation God wants to bestow upon you. But understand this one fact, righteousness is the foundation. If you don't know that you have righteousness, you will have no faith when you confess the promises of God. You won't really believe that God will give His blessings to you because your faith has been based on your good works.

When you understand righteousness, when you understand the incredible fact that you stand before God without any guilt or inferiority, you will automatically believe. Your faith will move you toward the promises of God in such a way that you will apprehend them, you will claim them, you will stand on them, and you will receive the mighty blessings of the Lord. You must understand that God views you as being perfectly righteous in Christ. Then you just begin to *say* it. You begin to say it to yourself, "I am righteous."

Now, when you begin to say that with your mouth, you must understand that the devil is terrified of your confession. He knows that he will lose his control over you and he will do everything he can to prevent you from saying it. Many believers will have certain thoughts come to them as they declare, "I am righteous." The devil will say, "How can you be righteous when you failed God yesterday, when you failed God this morning, when you failed God last week or last month?" He continually reminds us of our failures, he heaps guilt upon our heads and gets us away from the confession of our righteousness.

It's not enough to believe it in our hearts, we've got to say it with our mouths. That is what Jesus meant in Matthew 12:37 when He said, "For by thy words thou shalt be justified [made righteous], and by thy words thou shalt be condemned."

You must speak your way into the reality of

the righteousness of God in Jesus Christ. Say it with your mouth, "Christ took my sin; He paid the penalty for my sin; He rose from the dead to be my righteousness. Therefore, I am righteous with the righteousness of Christ." Say it again, *"I am righteous with the righteousness of Christ."*

The Divine Exchange

In 2 Corinthians 5:21 we read, "For he (God) hath made him (Jesus) to be sin for us, who knew no sin; that we might be made the righteousness of God in him." *This is the divine exchange.* God put your sin on Jesus. Your sin killed Him. My sin killed Him. Jesus took the sin of the entire world upon Himself on the cross. But then God took the righteousness that was in Christ and gave it to us. A divine exchange! He took our sin, gave it to Jesus, took His righteousness, and in turn, gave that back to us. That means *all His righteousness*—total, complete, everything—100 percent! When God looks at you He sees you in Jesus' righteousness.

There is a great verse in Revelation 12 that relates to this subject of declaring our righteousness. In verse 11 we read, "...they overcame him (Satan) by the blood of the Lamb, and by the word of their testimony; and they loved not their lives unto the death."

In verse 10 of the same chapter Satan is called "the accuser of our brethren...which accused them before our God day and night." Satan's job is to accuse you to yourself. His job is to accuse you to your brothers, sisters, parents, husband, or wife. Satan is the accuser. That's what he does best.

Revelation 12 is speaking of a future event. There is coming a time when believers are going to be responsible for the casting down of Satan. Notice how they will do it. The Bible says they accomplish it by the Blood of the Lamb and by the word of their testimony. They testified to what the Word said that the Blood did for them. When they gave that testimony in unity against the devil, the accuser of the brethren was cast down by Michael and the angels of heaven.

I believe it is the business of the Church to clear the second heaven of the devil and his angels. Notice what Jesus said in Matthew 28:18, 19:

18 ...All power is given unto me in heaven and in earth.
19 Go ye therefore...

He was transmitting His authority to the Church. He was telling us to go into the earth and into heaven as well. But that authority was not only authority on earth, which is what most men teach today, but I believe that authority is also in heaven—the second heaven.

When Jesus said, "Whatsoever you bind on earth will be bound in heaven," He was referring to the second heaven. There is a way you and I can bind Satan in the second heaven. We can take authority over him. Here is how we do it! By giving testimony to what the Word says about the Blood. In other words, we have to make our mouths testify. By your words you are made righteous; by your words you are condemned.

Believer's Authority

God has committed to believers on earth the ability to pull down the kingdom of Satan. I don't believe the Church is going to leave this world in the midst of great defeat. I believe we are going to establish the Kingdom of God in heaven and in earth by casting down the kingdom of Satan. But we must give testimony to what the Blood does for us.

What does the Word say about the action of the Blood on our behalf? *One great verse that I repeat to myself everyday* is Romans 5:9, "Much more then, being now justified by his blood, we shall be saved from wrath through him [Having now been made righteous by His Blood]." Your righteousness comes to you because of the action of the Blood of Jesus Christ. When Christ shed His Blood, He brought that Blood into the throne room before God.

Hebrews 9:12 documents this truth. He offered His Blood on the altar before God. That Blood is there today as freshly slain as when Jesus died on the cross 2,000 years ago. It is that Blood that covers your sin. When God looks at the Blood, He sees you through the Blood. He sees you as being righteous. He sees you clothed in the righteousness of His Son, Jesus Christ. We must declare this with our mouths.

This is the only way the Church is going to overcome the devil. This is the only way the Church is ever going to move in great faith and great power. The Church must accept the gift of righteousness obtained by the shedding of the Blood of Jesus Christ. It must give testimony to it. It must say it with its mouth. When it does, the power of Satan will be cast down.

But here is the problem, we can't believe God when there is condemnation and guilt inside of us. We can't believe God when Satan is pointing his finger at us and we are listening to the thoughts he fires at our minds every day. *Guilt rises up; it defeats us from within.* We have no real ability to enter into praise. We are unable to lift up the Name of the Lord with great power and great faith. We must eliminate that guilt. It must be taken care of.

Moving Out of Guilt

How can I move out of the guilt Satan has put upon me? Romans 4:5 gives us the key: "...to him that worketh not, but believeth on him that justifieth the ungodly, his faith is counted [reckoned] for righteousness." We don't work at it; we simply believe it! We have to believe that we are made righteous. Hallelujah! There comes a moment when you've got to break out of the prison of religion. You've got to break out of the prison of cultural doctrines that have bound you and held you. You've got to declare it with your lips before God, the devil, and mankind: *"I am righteous because God has made me righteous in Christ."*

There is a moment when that happens. You declare it boldly. When you do, something happens on the inside. You start it first with your mouth, you say it continually with your mouth. You confess it with your mouth and sooner or later your heart starts to pick it up.

Most religious people will hesitate at this point; it sounds presumptuous for a man to say, "I am righteous." Most of us who have been raised in the church have been made to feel guilty. Most preachers feel that in order to have any effect upon a congregation they have to preach guilt at them—and sin. In fact, many of the hymns of the Church are created to make us feel guilty. The righteousness of Jesus Christ is what will tear down the kingdom of Satan.

With your mouth, with your words, with your personal declaration, you can stand. You can say, "Lord, I believe that Jesus died as my personal representative. I believe He bore all my guilt and sin and condemnation. He died in my place and rose from the dead. Because I believe this, your Word tells me that the righteousness of Christ is now imputed to me and I receive it now as a free gift by believing in my heart. And I declare with my mouth that I am justified. I declare with my mouth that I am made righteous, just as if I had never sinned. Father, I thank you for this."

When you move into this position of righteousness, you will sense the praise of the Lord rising in your heart. Praise begins to move from the innermost part of your being. You become overwhelmed with the majesty, the awesome power of the grace of God—how God could count you righteous; how God could make you one-hundred-percent righteous in spite of your sin!

This is a mystery that is rooted in the heart and the love of God. When you see this in its depths, praise begins to spring forth from your heart. A love for God, like nothing you have ever known before in your life, begins to explode inside of your being. This is what praise is, this is the heart of praise. Only when you have seen righteousness can you truly un-derstand the full dimensions of what praise to God is.

When we understand righteousness, healing will come. Prosperity will be heaped upon us from the heavenly Father. We will move into deliverance from the strongholds of the devil that would attach them-selves to us. When you see—really *see*—what I have discussed in this chapter, your faith will never be the same again. Praise—the confession of the believer to the goodness of God—will lead you into powerful faith.

6

The Words of Our Mouths

Our Mouths—The Believer's Launching Pad

In examining the four launching rockets of the believer that we mentioned earlier, one important fact comes to light. Every one of the rockets is launched with the human mouth. We *pray* with our mouths, we *preach* with our mouths, we *testify* with our mouths and we *praise and worship* with our mouths. The mouth of the believer is the launching pad for the rockets of God. With our mouths, we can launch God's rockets or the devil's rockets. It is up to us to make the choice.

The Bible says, "And I saw three unclean spirits like frogs coming out of the *mouth* of the dragon, out of the *mouth* of the beast and out of the *mouth* of the false prophet, for they are spirits of demons performing signs which go out to the kings of the earth and of the whole world to gather them to the battle of that great day of God Almighty" (Rev. 16:13). Notice what John the Beloved saw: unclean spirits, like frogs, coming out of the mouth.

The mouths of the beast, the dragon, and the false prophet were the launching pads for unclean spirits that came out like frogs. It is interesting that John uses the comparison of frogs. Frogs make a croaking, monotonous, non-melodious sound. Every time I go behind the Iron Curtain and read a Soviet newspaper, I am reminded of the sound of frogs. The propaganda all sounds the same, there is no melody or harmony to it. It is just like the unclean spirit that came out of the mouth of the beast. It sounded like frogs.

This makes one point stand out for us: *our mouths are the center of spiritual warfare for the entire universe.* What incredible potential we carry in our mouths.

The devil is after our mouths; God is after our mouths. When Satan attacks us, he attacks us with thought bombs. He endeavors to establish a stronghold in our lives through the process of our thoughts. He wants his evil thoughts to capture our hearts. He wants those thoughts to go down inside of us. He wants them to be something we believe in, meditate upon and accept. The final goal of the devil is to get hold of our mouths.

Once our mouths are captured, Satan knows our mouths will speak out of the abundance of our hearts. When he has control of our mouths, he has control of us! He is able to launch his rockets. When our mouths are gossiping, backbiting, full of hatred, fear, lies, and so on, we are establishing Satan's kingdom with our mouths. It is easy to understand why the devil is after our mouths. He knows that his ability is limited to what he can get us to say. Think about that fact for a moment.

The Power of Confession

By the same token, God's goal is to get hold of our mouths. In a previous chapter I dealt with the power of confession in the mouth of the believer. We saw how we can change our hearts and minds by changing the words of our mouths. In the Hebrew language, the phrase, "to learn by heart" actually is translated "to learn by mouth," and this is how we learn best. We learned the poems of our youth, the multiplication tables, etc. by repeating them over and over again with our mouths. When we did this, we got to know them by heart. The words we spoke had great power in planting these things deep inside of us.

It is interesting to notice the connection between God's mouth and His Word in the Scriptures. The Bible says, "It is written, Man shall not live by bread alone, but by every word that proceedeth out of the mouth of God" (Matt. 4:4). The verb "proceedeth" in that verse is in the ever present tense. There is a word that is proceeding out of the mouth of God to us *right now.* That word carries God's creative power.

Isaiah 55:11 says, "So shall my word be that goeth forth out of my mouth: it shall not return unto me void, but it shall accomplish that which I please, and it shall prosper in the thing whereto I sent it." God's words out of God's mouth contain the creative power of the universe. We have the potential of that same creative power when we put God's words in our mouths. The words you speak with your mouth will deliver you or put you in bondage. "For by thy words thou shalt be justified, and by thy words thou shalt be condemned" (Matt. 12:37).

The Bible says, "The mouth of a righteous man is a well of life..." (Prov. 10:11). Proverbs 12:14 says, "A man shall be satisfied with good by the fruit of his mouth..." Most believers have no idea of the power they carry in their mouths. The words we put into our mouths are like seeds; they produce after their kind. We plant them in the ground when we say them. We are going to reap a harvest from the words we have spoken. Therefore, it is vital for us to learn to speak the kind of words that are going to bring a good harvest.

It is imperative, also, for us to have a Biblical understanding of the power of God's words. The Bible says that God is upholding all things by the word of His power (see Heb. 1:3). Not only did God speak everything into existence by His words, but He is upholding and maintaining the operation of His creation by the same word of His power. Hebrews 11:3 says that "the worlds were framed by the word of God...."

The Power of Our Words

God has designed our mouths so as to flow in the course of God's creativity. Notice the power of the words of Jesus in Mark 11:12-14; Jesus was hungry and He saw a fig tree. When He came close to the fig tree, He found that there were no figs on it, only leaves. In response, Jesus said to the fig tree, "No man eat fruit of thee hereafter for ever." He spoke mere words to the tree. The next morning as they passed by the fig tree, Peter noticed it was dried up from the roots. He spoke to Jesus and said, "...Master, behold, the fig tree which thou cursedst is withered away" (verse 21).

How did Jesus curse? He simply said to the fig tree, "No man eat fruit of thee hereafter for ever." His words contained a negative power to destroy the life in that tree. His words were literally a curse to that tree.

Most believers don't realize that we curse when we speak negatively against someone with our words. We think we have free rein to talk about them as we will.

I remember a particular incident when I was growing up. A sinner in the community came to church, repented before God, and confessed his sins. Someone in the congregation said, "Well, I know him pretty well; it may last for two or three weeks, but soon he'll be back doing the same thing; you watch." Their words took on the form of a curse; they hadn't meant to curse the man, but they did nonetheless.

Sure enough, just as they had prophesied, in three weeks, he was back doing the same things again.

Always remember this about the words of your mouth; *they have creative power.* They will create either good or evil. The power of creativity is in your mouth. That is why both God and the devil are after the words of your mouth. Satan has one major strategy in relation to your mouth. He is determined to make you doubt God's Word.

Hath God Said

When Adam and Eve were placed by God in the Garden, God told them they were not to eat of the fruit that came from the tree of the knowledge of good and evil (see Genesis 3). Satan knew that in tempting Adam and Eve, he had to get them to doubt God's Word concerning that tree. When he came to Eve in the Garden, he asked, *"...hath God said..."?* Satan placed a question mark in the mind of Eve. He said, "Hath God indeed said you shall not eat this fruit?" (my paraphrase). Then he tried to interpret what God meant when He said, "Thou shall not eat thereof."

In verse 4 and 5 he says to Eve,

4 ...Ye shall not surely die;
5 For God doth know that in the day ye eat thereof, then your eyes shall be opened, and ye shall be as gods, knowing good and evil.

He was subtle in the way he approached Eve. He is subtle in the way he approaches you and me. And yet his tactics have not changed. He is committed to getting you to doubt what God has said. He says to you and me, "Maybe God's Word means what it says, maybe it doesn't. There is a 50-50 chance that this is exactly what God meant. Or, *maybe, He meant something else?"*

God's Word requires absolute obedience. Satan

would attempt to introduce situational ethics to our response; he would whisper in our ear and say God's Word doesn't mean to be absolute. "Sometime God heals, but not all the time. His Word may heal you today, but it may not work next week."

His job is merely to put a question mark in our minds. When he has created doubt inside of us, then he has robbed us of the power of God's spoken Word. That is his first step. Once he has made us doubt the absolute character of God's Word, then he takes the second step. He gets us to express our doubts with our mouths. We pray and ask God to do something but when it appears that nothing is happening we change our prayers and begin to complain to the Lord by saying, "God, it is not working out." That is precisely what Satan wants you to say. You are making your words line up with his. *You have just spoken creatively on Satan's behalf.*

In the natural, it appears obvious that things are not working out, but if you are standing on the promises of God, God's Word says they will work out. We have to make our words line up with God rather than the devil.

Many of us have been saying what the devil says for years. We've complained before the Lord and said, "I've prayed about this sickness and I'm not getting better, I'm only getting worse." We have our eyes on the symptoms, on the way we see, hear and feel, rather than on the truth of the Word of God. Then we allow our words to line up with what the devil says. We have literally bound ourselves with the words of our mouths, then we place the blame on God.

When we get out of faith in our praying, there is no believing. We think God has forsaken us. When we make a mistake and fail to hear the voice of God in a certain situation, it is so easy for the devil to convince us that we have failed the Lord. He is a master at this, believe me. He will do everything he can to heap guilt upon you. He will point to the fact that if you had listened to God, you wouldn't have gotten into this problem. He'll tell you that God is mad at you and that God is going to let you stew for a while to make you suffer. But that is not the way God conducts His business.

God's Will For You Is Blessing

There is one foundation of faith that must be established in your life at this point. God is a good God; the devil is evil. God does not want you to be in poverty. He does not want you to be sick. He does not want your marriage to fall apart. ***God's will for you is blessing.*** Jesus said, "The thief cometh not, but for to steal, and to kill, and to destroy: I am come that they might have life, and that they might have it more abundantly" (John 10:10). Jesus came to give us life and everything that goes with having an abundant life. The thief comes to take it away from us.

Jesus said that He had come to destroy the works of the devil. The devil has set his face against you. A lot of people pray to God out of one side of their mouths and ask God to prosper them; then with the other side of their mouths, they put their financial affairs under the control of the devil by saying that everything is going wrong.

As a believer, you must become aware of the fact that you are engaged in spiritual warfare. This is not a fairy tale conflict with mythological characters. You are under an attack of the devil. He has demon spirits that know you better than you know yourself. They are experts at manipulating your thoughts. They are doing everything they can to create words in your mouth that will bind you for the rest of your life. Until we see this, it is impossible to come into the power of God through the use of our mouths.

Delegated Authority

It is vital for us to understand God's delegated authority at this point. In Matthew 28:18, 19 Jesus gave the disciples the Great Commission:

> **18 ...All power is given unto me in heaven and in earth.**
> **19 Go ye therefore, and teach all nations...**

In these verses He is delegating the authority that had been given to Him in heaven and in earth to the Church. He is telling us to go into all the earth, to make disciples of all nations.

He then goes on to tell us in Mark 16:17, 18:

> **17 ...these signs shall follow them that believe; In my name shall they cast out devils; they shall speak with new tongues;**
> **18 ...they shall lay hands on the sick, and they shall recover.**

God has delegated to us the power and authority to establish His Kingdom in heaven and on earth. However, most believers have never seen this. They continue to ask God to do something about the devil. They do not understand that God has done everything about the devil He's ever going to do. He finished that work through His Son, Jesus Christ, on the cross. Satan's power is destroyed and God is waiting for the church to exercise its authority.

God has established important principles in the area of authority. First, when authority is given, responsibility is demanded. You cannot have authority without having responsibility for the proper use of that authority. When God gave us authority over the devil, He expected us to be responsible for doing something about the devil. God won't do it; He is waiting for us to do it. Because God has delegated His authority to us, we are expected to use it. It is our responsibility to do so.

God knows that we stand as His authority here on the earth. When we, as His authority, speak Satan's words out of our mouths, we establish Satan's authority in our lives. We establish his disease in our bodies. We establish his bondage in our finances. We establish his divorce in our marriage. Because God has delegated His authority to us, we are responsible for our words. This is a great spiritual key!

It is useless for you to ask God to prosper you when your words are constantly speaking poverty. When we allow our words to line up with what the devil is saying, then by the power of our mouths we make it impossible for God to work. We bind Him by the words of our mouths. That is an awesome fact that many believers have to see.

When you pray to God and say, "Lord, I asked you to help me but it's not working," you make your words agree with the enemy. In so doing, you also make it impossible for God to help you. You have taken the authority that was delegated to you and have put it under the control of Satan. Things will not change until you change the words of your mouth. God meant for you to exercise dominion with the words of your mouth. Your mouth is the key. Until you begin to speak God's Word, the situation will remain the same.

Matthew 12:37 says it so well, "For by thy words thou shalt be justified, and by thy words thou shalt be condemned." Proverbs 18:21 says, "Death and life are in the power of the tongue: and they that love it shall eat the fruit thereof." Because of the authority God has placed within us, our mouths can speak death or our mouths can speak life. We are responsible for the words that come out of our mouths. Matthew 12:35 says, "A good man out of the good treasure of his heart bringeth forth good things..." Proverbs 10:11 says, "The mouth of a righteous man is a well of life..."

The words of our mouths have creative power. The devil tries to get us to say what he wants us to say. God doesn't cause our sickness or financial problems. They come from the fact that we are under attack from the devil. We have bound what God can do with our words. He would have to violate His delegation of authority in order to help us in such a case. He would have to override the authority He gave us when He said, "All power is given unto me in heaven and earth, go ye therefore" (see Matt. 28:18, 19).

Faith is God's Way

God insists that we work according to His rules. It is no good for Him to heal us or to bless us financially if that healing does not come through the right channel. He demands that we come to Him through the avenue of faith. Hebrews 11:6 says, "But without faith it is impossible to please him: for he that cometh to God must believe that he is, and that he is a rewarder of them that diligently seek him."

God is a faith God. He refuses to operate any other way. When we beg for divine blessing and violate the authority given to us by the words of our mouths, He will not bless us until we get our words in line with His words. It would weaken you for the rest of your life if He allowed prosperity to come to you because you begged Him a couple of times in prayer. First, He must teach you the principles of how prosperity comes. He must teach you the principles of how healing comes. You must get the words of your mouth lined up with the Word of God, then these blessings can be yours.

If you are speaking unbelief, if your words are lined up with what the devil is trying to do to you, then He would have to contradict His principles in order to intervene in your life. That is why our mouths are vital to God's blessing in our lives.

It is like learning how to get strong by exercising your muscles. If you lie in bed and ask your mother to do everything for you, your muscles get weak and atrophy. The time comes when you must get up and begin to do things for yourself. This is what God is asking us to do. He is demanding that we resist the devil. He is demanding that we stand against poverty, that we resist disease, that we resist his attack on our families, on our children, on our loved ones, on our physical bodies.

God knows that the only way you'll get strong is by resisting, even though it makes us feel incredibly vulnerable. We think God has forgotten us. We beg and cry and plead and say, "Lord, please help me." And He replies, "I have already helped you in my Word. My strength and power are in my Word."

He tells us, "My divine power has already given to you everything that pertains to life and godliness, therefore I have given to you exceeding great and precious promises that by these you may be partakers of the divine nature" (see 2 Pet. 1:3, 4)

Through the Word of God we can hear Jesus saying, "I've already provided the healing, I've already provided the financial blessing, I've already provided the turnaround in your relationships. My promises are there, but you must make your mouth line up with the promises I have given."

When I come under attack in a certain area of my life, I make a list of promises that deal with the specific problem. I then take the promises and put them on Scripture cards and begin to meditate on those promises. When I say them to myself, and sing them to myself, those promises begin to explode in my spirit and the Word of God brings me into a powerful faith.

Praising God With The Promises

This is a real key for believers in learning how to praise God with the promises. We must learn to stand on the fact that God's promises are true and even though we cannot see the answer at a given point, He is blessing us and supplying all of our needs according to His riches in glory. He has healed us through the work of His Son on Calvary 2,000 years ago. As we take our stand with the promises and make those promises come out of our mouths, we begin to release faith. Faith begins to stir inside of us. Faith begins to explode in our spirits. Faith begins to rise up against the mountains of the devil.

Then we find ourselves moving into the answer from God. It is important to realize, however, that you don't make this kind of thing happen by trying it once or twice. It doesn't happen in an hour. When you take the Word of God that speaks about healing or financial blessing, you are bringing the Word of God against your own cultural tradition that has been built up over the last twenty or thirty years.

It's going to take some time for the reeducation process to take place. You must stand with the Word of God in the midst of all of the circumstantial evidence to the contrary. When things look like they are falling apart all around you, you have to declare that God's Word is truth, that God is supplying all your needs according to His riches in glory. What you are doing in this case is training your spirit with the Word of God. You are training your inner man, and this is going to take some time.

We live in a quick-fix society. We want instant everything—instant breakfast, instant medicine, instant relief, instant pleasure, instant money. But this process of standing on God's Word will take some time. Remember the story of my wife Shirley. It took her over a year and a half to receive the answer.

What Does the Word Say?

The Bible says, "This book of the law shall not depart out of thy mouth..." (Josh. 1:8). You've got to keep the Word of God in your mouth. The passage goes on to say, "...but thou shalt meditate therein day and night, that thou mayest observe to do according to all that is written therein: for then thou shalt make thy way prosperous, and then thou shalt have good success." There is no better way to come into the blessings of God. Your mouth is the key.

Psalm 1:1-3 says:

1 Blessed is the man...
2 (whose) delight is in the law of the Lord; and in his law doth he meditate day and night.
3 ...he shall be like a tree planted by the rivers of water, that bringeth forth his fruit in his season; his leaf also shall not wither; and whatsoever he doeth shall prosper.

You have to stay with it. Our delight has to be in the Word of God. We must meditate on it day and night.

Notice the instruction Solomon gives in Proverbs 4:20-22:

20 My son, attend to my words; incline thine ear unto my sayings.
21 Let them not depart from thine eyes; keep them in the midst of thine heart.
22 For they are life unto those that find them, and health to all their flesh.

Notice he says, "Attend to my words...incline thine ear...let them not depart...keep them." See how important this reeducation process is!

Remember, the secret of faith is continually saying with your mouth what God is saying in His Word. *If you will stay with it, and keep saying it, sooner or later, there is going to be a release of*

faith in your inner man. You're going to come into an awareness and full assurance that God is going to honor His Word in your life in regard to healing, finances or whatever.

You will break into a realm of faith you never knew existed. When you come into this kind of faith, you will start to praise God because you know you already have the answer. Your praise will release the energy for the fulfillment of everything God is doing within you. My brother, my sister, ***you've got it.***

7

How God's Word Works

In this book I have made some very bold statements concerning the Word of God. I have told you that "every word that God speaks contains the power in itself for its own fulfillment." There is a powerful life; an all-encompassing energy in God's Word. In this chapter I want to look again at the term "The Word of God"—what does it mean? Then I want to examine what the Word of God does. What kind of effects does God's Word produce? We often say—the Word works! My question is *how does it work?*

The Living Word

What or who exactly is the Word of God? In the original Greek the word used is *logos.* This term is used in the Gospel of John and the Epistle to the Hebrews more than it is used in the other books of the New Testament, but the two writers use the term in reference to different things or beings.

John uses the term in reference to the person of Jesus Christ. For example, in John 1:1, 2 we read:

1 In the beginning was the Word, and the Word was with God, and the Word was God.
2 The same was in the beginning with God.

Verse 14 goes on, "And the Word was made flesh, and dwelt among us, (and we beheld his glory as of the only begotten of the Father,) full of grace and truth." It is obvious from these words that John is referring to the person of Jesus Christ.

Jesus and The Word Are One

However, the term "the Word of God" is used by the writer to the Hebrews to refer to something different. Hebrews 4:12 says, "...the word of God is quick, and powerful..." This term, "the Word of God," refers to the written Scriptures, or the Bible. This may appear to be a conflict on the surface. (Would the real Word of God please stand up!)

Is Jesus Christ the Word of God or is your Bible the Word of God? The answer is really very simple. They both are the Word of God! The Bible is the record of what God has said in a book. In essence, they are one and the same.

Only when you approach your Bible on the basis of this fact, will it become alive for you the way God means for it to be alive. This is precisely what Jesus meant in John 6:63 when He said, "It is the spirit that quickeneth; the flesh profiteth nothing..." Notice the next sentence also, "...the words that I speak unto you, they are spirit, and they are life." Jesus said that His words are spirit.

In John 4:24 Jesus said, "God is a Spirit: and they that worship him must worship him in spirit and in truth." What is Jesus referring to here by His use of the word "spirit"? John 6:63 states that His words are spirit. John 4:24 says "God is a Spirit." Do you see the connection?

God and the words of Jesus are one and the same. They have the same essence—the same divine nature—*Zoe.* Many of us have found this very difficult to believe, and yet, it is precisely at this point that you either catch the revelation of the meaning and the power of the Word of God, or you lose it.

Receiving the Word of God

Paul writes these words to the church in Thessalonica, "For this cause also thank we God without ceasing, because, when ye receive the word of God which ye heard of us, ye received it not as the word of men, but as it is in truth, the word of God, which effectually worketh also in you that believe" (1 Thess. 2:13). Notice several things about this verse. Paul is thankful beyond measure; because, when the Thessalonians heard him preach the Word of God, they received it not as the word of a man, but, as it is in truth, the Word of God.

Now that's an awesome statement. Paul was a man like any one of us. I'm sure the Thessalonians were tempted, as are most congregations in America, to measure a minister by the clothes he wears, by the flow of his oratory, by the color of his tie, or the way he combs his hair. But these Thessalonians were able to see past the superficial. They listened to the words coming out of Paul's mouth, not as the words of a man; but, as they were—truly, the Word of God. Paul was saying to them, "It was God's Word coming out of my mouth, and you received it as God's Word. And then, because you received it as God's Word, *it effectually worked in you that believed."*

"Effectually worketh" comes from the same word translated "powerful" in Hebrews 4:12, *energes.* He said, "This word that I preach to you was powerful in you. *It worked.* It created the energy and life of God in you. Because you received it not from me, as my words, but, as it was in truth, the Word of God."

I have reemphasized these truths because I feel they are so fundamental to our understanding of the subject of faith. This Word of God will create and do in you the same thing it did in the Thessalonian believers. *It effectually works!* It is possible, however, to miss the working of God's Word. We can render it ineffective by the manner in which we receive

God's Word. The believers in Thessalonica believed, and because they believed, it worked. If you don't believe, it won't work.

The next question is, "What happens when the Word works?" What kind of effects does God's Word produce? The first effect God's Word produces in the life of the believer is faith. The Bible says "So then faith cometh by hearing, and hearing by the word of God" (Rom. 10:17).

Faith

What does the word "faith" mean? In general conversation we use this word quite often. We may speak of having faith in a medicine or faith in a parent, faith in a teacher or in a politician. The word "faith," as it is used in Scripture, however, must be defined in a more accurate manner.

Romans 10:17 tells us that faith comes from hearing the Word of God, so faith has to be directly related to God's Word. Faith comes only from God's Word. Bible faith is not believing anything you want to. Bible faith is defined as: believing that God means what He has said in His Word, or believing He will do as He has promised in His Word.

David exercised faith when he said unto the Lord, "Therefore now, Lord, let the thing that thou hast spoken concerning thy servant and concerning his house be established forever, and *do as thou hast said*" (1 Chron. 17:23, italics mine). That phrase defines what faith is.

Mary responded in almost the same way as David did. Do you remember when the angel came and announced to her that she would bear the child Jesus? Her reply to the angel was very simple, "...be it unto me according to thy word..." (Luke 1:38). She is actually saying the same thing David did. David said, "Do as thou hast said." Mary said, "Be it unto me according to thy word." This is real New

Testament faith.

It is important to note that faith—real Bible faith—is basic to any transaction between God and man. You can't communicate or do business with God without faith. Hebrews 11:6 is clear on this point, "But without faith it is impossible to please him: for he that cometh to God must believe that he is, and that he is a rewarder of them that diligently seek him."

If you are going to come to God, you have to believe. Faith is the first thing God demands from you in your approach to Him. And the only way to get that faith is to come to the Word of God. Faith cometh by hearing, and hearing by the Word of God.

Let us examine the essence of faith more thoroughly. The eleventh chapter of Hebrews is the classic Bible chapter on faith. The first verse of the chapter gives us a definition of what faith is. It says, "Now faith is the substance of things hoped for, the evidence of things not seen." This verse makes two statements concerning faith.

First, faith is the substance of things hoped for. Faith is so real in God's world that it is actually a substance. The Greek word for substance is ***hupostasis.*** It simply means: "something that provides the basis or foundation for." We may say that faith is the underlying reality of things hoped for, the foundation of things hoped for. It is real. It is a substance.

Faith Sees the Invisible

Second, faith is the evidence of things not seen. So it is clear that *faith relates to the unseen world, to the invisible.* This is a very important point concerning faith. Faith relates us to the unseen world.

The Scriptures say, "Through faith we understand that the worlds were framed by the word of God, so that things which are seen were made of things which do not appear" (Heb. 11:3). In other words, God made the visible (that which we can see) out of the invisible (that which we cannot see). Faith takes us behind the curtain of the visible and lets us see the invisible. And, *the foundation for that invisible world is the Word of God.* Ponder that if you will.

This creates a natural tension in every one of us. It is only natural for a man to believe what he can see. We are taught that in our educational processes, "Don't believe anything that you cannot experiment with in a test tube and prove to be correct," the professor says. But, the Bible approaches the subject from a totally different angle.

Paul says, "For we walk by faith, not by sight" (2 Cor. 5:7). This verse illustrates that tension. It's very difficult for a man to walk by faith; he rather wants to walk by sight. But if we are going to walk by faith, we don't need sight. The one excludes the other.

A lot of us subscribe to the proverb that says, "I'm from Missouri and I've got to be shown." In other words, seeing is believing. But the Bible reverses the order. First, we must believe; then we will see. David makes this principle very clear. He says, "I had fainted, unless I had believed to see the goodness of the Lord in the land of the living" (Ps. 27:13). Another translation says, "I would have despaired, unless I had believed that I would see the goodness of the Lord in the land of the living."

Notice, he had to believe before he could see, and, that's true for every one of us. We have to believe we are going to see the Lord's goodness before it actually manifests itself. This stops us from despairing.

Believe, Then See

This New Testament principle is clarified in the

story of Jesus raising Lazarus from the dead. We read in John 11:39, 40:

> **39 Jesus said, Take ye away the stone. Martha, the sister of him that was dead, saith unto him, Lord, by this time he stinketh: for he hath been dead four days.**
> **40 Jesus saith unto her, Said I not unto thee, that, *if thou wouldest believe, thou shouldest see the glory of God?*** (italics mine)

Another translation puts it this way, "Did I not say to you, ***if you believe, you will see*** the glory of God." The principle is the same: First we believe, then we see. Faith comes before sight.

You can understand this principle in your rational mind. But, understanding it in your spirit is another thing altogether. Our old nature wants to see. It simply does not want to ***believe.*** Our new nature has to believe first in order to see.

So this tremendous conflict is going on inside of us all the time. Faith that comes from the Word of God determines that it does not need to see, but, it will rather believe first. And because it believes first, then it will see. ***You've got to believe you are healed of a disease before you see yourself healed.*** You've got to believe you are prospered by the Word of God before you see yourself prospered. You've got to believe that you have victory over the devil before it is evident that the victory is there. ***That is faith.***

Paul was certainly aware of this challenge in his own ministry. He defines it so clearly for us in 2 Corinthians 4:17, 18:

> **17 For our light affliction, which is but for a moment, worketh for us a far more exceeding and eternal weight of glory;**
> **18 While we look not at the things which are seen, but at the things which are not seen: for the**

things which are seen are temporal; but the things which are not seen are eternal.

On the surface Paul's words don't make any sense. Verse 18 says, "While we look not at the things which are seen, but at the things which are not seen." How can you look at things which are not seen? If you can't see them, how can you look at them? Faith is the way we look at the unseen. *Faith is the way we look into the eternal realities of God's world.*

God wants us at home in His world. He has given us this great avenue of faith so that we can live and operate as He lives and operates. When you have faith, you will be able to see the realities of God's invisible world, and they will be as real to you as anything that you can see with your natural eyes. Praise the Lord!

Jesus said, "...with God all things are possible" (Matt. 19:26). In Mark 9:23 we read His words again, "...all things are possible to him that believeth." Notice the similarity between these two verses. Both verses contain the phrase, "all things are possible."

Now that's not hard for us to believe. Obviously, our God is a big God and everything's possible to Him. But, notice what Mark is saying, "...all things are possible to him that believeth." What does that mean? If we have faith, we can do what God does. *The things that are possible to God become possible to man through faith.* Through faith, all that is possible to God becomes equally possible to us.

Can you see why the Bible emphasizes the subject of faith so repetitively? *Faith is fundamental— absolutely fundamental for your life and mine.*

Hope vs. Faith

It is impossible to discuss the subject of faith without discussing the subject of hope. There is a great difference between these two words that most believers have not been able to discern.

Hope is a counterfeit of faith. Hoping will not bring a miracle to pass in your life. Believing will get it done. You can hope from now to eternity to have the money to meet a certain obligation and you'll never have it. Faith has it now.

One of the best ways to study faith is to define hope, because hope will tell you what faith is not. Faith takes hold of the unrealities of hope and it brings them into the realm of reality now. You don't hope for healing, because you'll never get it that way. You have to believe it's yours and then you'll have it.

Please don't misunderstand me. Hope has its place in the life of the New Testament believer, but we must be careful not to mistake our hope for faith.

The primary difference between faith and hope is that faith is in the heart and hope is in the mind. Paul said, "For with the heart man believeth unto righteousness" (Rom. 10:10). Notice the preposition "unto." It denotes progress or motion forward. When you have faith in your heart it is never quiet, it is never static, it is always active, it is always moving. If you believe, you'll be changed by what you believe. But, notice, **faith works in the heart not in the head.** It has to get into your heart.

Many people accept the truth of God's Word intellectually. They will agree to the doctrine expressed by the truth of God's Word. But mental acceptance of truth is not faith. Faith, to be effective, is believed on in the heart. Only when it gets into your heart will it work. Faith is something you may never understand with your mind, but your heart knows when you've got it. Hope is something else.

Paul says, "But let us, who are of the day, be sober, putting on the breastplate of faith and love; and for an helmet, the hope of salvation" (1 Thess.

5:8). Hope is God's helmet that protects your head or your mind. As believers, we are counseled to wear the helmet of hope twenty-four hours a day.

What exactly is hope? Hope may be defined as: believing that the best is yet to be, all things are working together for good, an optimistic outlook that believes that God's blessings are coming to you. Hope refuses to dwell on the negative. It protects the mind from the subtle attacks of the devil. It is more than just the use of positive thinking.

It is based on what the Bible teaches us about God. God is causing all things to work together for our good. That is a fact. Hope believes in that fact. This makes it impossible for a good Christian to be a pessimist. If you are looking on the bad side and negative side all the time, you are not exercising Biblical hope. You are allowing the devil to undermine the thought of your mind. But, notice, even hope finds its foundation in the Word of God.

I Hoped for a Wife

Let me explain this from my own personal experience. Several years ago, as I mentioned earlier, I went through a severe tragedy in my life. I was told that my late wife had been killed in a car accident in Tulsa. It is impossible to describe the pain, the hurt and anger I experienced.

Through praise, God ministered to me in a powerful way and led me into the ministry of praise and worship. As I entered into this new ministry in praise, I sensed in my heart that God did not want me to remain single for the rest of my life. I had three children at home without a mother. And, on the basis of Romans 8:28, I believed that all things were going to work together for good in my life. However, I sensed that I needed to wait some time before I remarried. I had the awareness that I was to wait two years before I made any effort to find another partner.

During that time period I went through many battles in my mind. The devil told me I would never find a wife. He told me that there were no women who would be willing to take on the responsibility of three children. He said, "Your travel and your lifestyle would scare any good woman away." And yet, I continued to hope with a confident, steady optimism that when the time was right, God would act. I knew that all things were working together for my good.

That is different than faith. **When you have faith, then you know you have it now.** But, I was hoping with a confident, steady optimism that when the two-year time period was up, the wife of my future would be there. When the two-year time period was up I met Shirley, the most beautiful lady in the whole world, at McDonald's. It was almost two years to the exact day. **That is the exercise of hope.**

Hope is Future

The second difference between faith and hope is the fact that **faith is in the present and hope is in the future.** Do you remember how we described faith as a substance, a foundation, something that is actual, something that is real. Hope is different. Hope is an expectation. When you have faith, you have it now. When you hope, you feel you will have it in the future.

Many of God's people are deceived at this point. They have mistaken their hope for faith. They will come to me in my meetings and say, "I have great faith. Pray for me for God to do this or that." As soon as they make that statement, I know they don't have faith. If they had faith, they would already have their request and they wouldn't have to ask me to pray for them. They have the two principles mixed up in their minds.

Because hope is in the mind, most people feel that they have faith. You can know what's in your mind, because your mind is aware of its own thoughts. But the thought that God is going to do something good for you is not faith—it is hope. Faith is in your heart. And, it's difficult to know sometimes when you really have faith.

There have been times when I have prayed for people and I felt nothing in the natural. In my mind, I was not aware of any faith at all inside of me. In a church in Medicine Hat, Alberta, Canada, where I was ministering several years ago some people brought a little baby into my meeting whom they had taken from the hospital. It was being fed intravenously. It had tubes in its nose, etc. When I looked at that child, I felt nothing in myself. I simply laid my hand on the child in obedience to the Word of God and prayed a simple prayer.

When I finished praying, I felt nothing. I walked away, saddened by the fact that I had not felt anything. You can imagine my surprise when several months later I found out that that child was instantly healed by the power of God. *Now I didn't feel any faith at all, but faith was in my heart, you see.* That's why so many of us are mistaken in the subject of faith.

Remember faith is today; hope is tomorrow. If you believe you'll be healed tomorrow, you have hope. If you believe you are healed now, then you have faith. That's the difference. No amount of re-programing of the mind can create faith in the mind. Faith happens in your heart. And faith comes from receiving the Word of God in your heart.

How To Receive Faith

We now come to the most important question concerning the subject of faith. *How can I get it?* Can I really have it myself? Is it just for great men of the Bible like Paul and Peter, David and Elijah, or is it for me? Should I just wait and allow God in His providence to drop faith into my heart when He wants to? Is there something I can do now to receive it?

"...without faith it is impossible to please him (God)" (Heb. 11:6). Therefore, you have to get it. You must receive it. You must have it or you'll never please Him. We are responsible to get faith. If you are responsible for getting faith, there must be a way it will come to you.

Our answer is found in Romans 10:17: "So then faith cometh by hearing, and hearing by the word of God." You may have read that verse a hundred times before; but, as you read it now, I want you to notice just one word—"cometh." Faith cometh. Can you see that? Faith comes to you as you hear God's Word. That means, you can get faith. How does it come? It comes simply when you hear the Word of God.

How Can I Hear?

The next question is: How can I hear God's Word? Solomon describes the process in Proverbs 4:20-22:

20 My son, attend to my words; incline thine ear unto my sayings.
21 Let them not depart from thine eyes; keep them in the midst of thine heart.
22 For they are life unto those that find them, and health to all their flesh.

Notice verse 22, where the writer of the Proverbs is telling us that in God's Word there is life. In God's Word there is health. Some translations put it "Medicine to all our flesh."

The two verses prior to verse 22 tell us how to find that life.

In verse 20 the writer says, "My son, attend." That is the first step we take in the process of hearing the Word of God. I must give undivided, concentrated attention to God's words as I read them. This also has the idea of spending time with God's Word.

The second instruction is to "incline thine ear." That means: to adopt a humble and teachable attitude. To lay aside preconceived doctrines and ideas. To subject your thinking to the power of what God's Word says.

The third instruction is, "Let them not depart from thine eyes." I must totally focus on what God says in His Word and not on what other writers may write in their books or articles. I must focus my eyes on the truth of what God says and not on the symptoms that are causing problems in my life.

The fourth instruction is, "Keep them in the midst of thine heart." This means, we are to do what Moses commanded Joshua, "This book of the law shall not depart out of thy mouth; but thou shalt meditate therein day and night" (Joshua 1:8). As I continue to meditate on the truth of God's Word and what God has said in His Word, the power and impact of God's Word will come to my heart.

This is how faith comes. It's not very complicated. In fact, *it's very simple.* First, I give undivided attention to God's Word. I bow before it and allow it to teach me. I keep my eyes focused on it no matter what comes against me. And, I always meditate on that Word in my heart day and night.

Isn't this what Paul told us to do in 2 Corinthians 4:18? He told us, "...look not at the things which are seen, but at the things which are not seen: for the things which are seen are temporal; but the things which are not seen are eternal." If we continue to look at the eternal realities of healing, of prosperity, of God's blessing in our lives; sooner or later the realities of the unseen world will manifest themselves in our bodies and in our personal circumstances. Praise the Lord!

In Romans 10:17 Paul says, "...faith cometh by hearing, and hearing by *the word* of God" (italics mine). He uses the word *rhema* for the term "the word."

Logos and Rhema

In the original Greek of the New Testament there are two different words, both of which are normally translated as "word." The first is *logos;* the second is *rhema.* There is a distinct difference in their meanings.

Logos is the unchanging, self-existent Word of God. David, speaking in Psalms 119:89, says, "For ever, O Lord, thy word is settled in heaven." God's Word has been in eternity past and will continue on into eternity future. It will never change. It is that total, unchanging Word of God.

The *rhema,* on the other hand, is derived from a verb meaning "to speak," and means specifically: *"a word that is spoken."* When Paul says, "...faith cometh by hearing, and hearing by the word of God," it is obvious that in order to be heard a word must be spoken. If we are going to hear that word, it must be spoken by the Holy Spirit.

The Bible contains the *logos,* the total Word of God. But it is vast and very complex. It is hard for me to understand it all. *Rhema is when the Holy Spirit takes a small portion of the logos, and speaks it into my heart in the midst of my human experience. Rhema* is a small part of *logos* that applies to my particular situation. It is spoken to me under the influence of the Holy Spirit.

That's what happens when you are reading a portion of the Scriptures that you may have read a hundred times before, and all of a sudden, it comes alive with a certain meaning that is special for you. The words are made alive by the power of the Holy Spirit. And your response at that point must be to hear. **Rhema** comes to each of us directly and individually from God the Holy Spirit.

An excellent example of the power of **rhema** is given in the words Jesus spoke to Satan in the wilderness! "...Man shall not live by bread alone, but by every word that proceedeth out of the mouth of God" (Matt. 4:4). The word "proceedeth" is in the continuing present tense in the Greek. Jesus tells us that there is a word proceeding directly and continually from God's mouth to us. It is energized by the power of the Holy Spirit. **It is a rhema word.** And this word is to be our daily bread. It's always fresh; it's always new. This is how a believer should live. As we continue to hear that **rhema** word, we live in the midst of powerful faith.

In Isaiah 55:8-11, Isaiah gives us a comparison of **logos** and **rhema:**

> **8 For my thoughts are not your thoughts, neither are your ways my ways, saith the Lord.**
> **9 For as the heavens are higher than the earth, so are my ways higher than your ways, and my thoughts than your thoughts.**
> **10 For as the rain cometh down, and the snow from heaven, and returneth not thither, but watereth the earth, and maketh it bring forth and bud, that it may give seed to the sower, and bread to the eater:**
> **11 So shall my word be that goeth forth out of my mouth: it shall not return unto me void, but it shall accomplish that which I please, and it shall prosper in the thing whereto I sent it.**

Here Isaiah is talking about the thoughts of God. As the heavens are higher than the earth, so His thoughts are higher than our thoughts. He is referring here to the total counsel of God settled forever in heaven. He is referring directly to the **logos.**

Rhema is the Rain

We are on another plane, however; we're living down here on earth. And our ways and thoughts are far below those of God. It is impossible for us to rise up to God's level on our own. So God sends His thoughts to us, like the rain and the snow that bring moisture upon the earth. Isaiah says, **"...as the rain cometh down,** ...and watereth the earth, and maketh it bring forth...that it may give seed to the sower, and bread to the eater..." In the next verse he continues, **"So shall my word be..."** That word that comes down to us out of heaven is the **rhema** Word of God. It is the spoken Word of God. It is that part of God's Word that applies to our particular situation and it meets the need we have at that precise moment.

Isaiah says, "...it (that word) shall prosper in the thing whereto I (God) sent it." **The Word does have the power for its own fulfillment.** Once faith has come to us through the **rhema** Word of God, then we are responsible for what we do with it. It is at this point that we must speak with our mouths, what God has spoken to us in our spirits. This is when we enter into the New Testament act of confession.

In previous chapters I discussed with you the fact that the sacrifice of praise is actually New Testament confession. Faith that does not speak is stillborn. If that **rhema** word has exploded in our hearts, we've got to say it. We've got to make the words of our mouths line up with the Word of God.

And this is essentially what praise is. Praise is an act of New Testament confession. We begin to praise the Lord for the fact that we are healed. We begin to praise the Lord that through the Word we are blessed financially. We begin to praise the Lord that we are experiencing victory over the devil. **Praise, therefore, becomes the release for our faith.**

The Word says, "For with the heart man believeth unto righteousness; and with the mouth confession is made unto salvation" (Rom. 10:10). When the **rhema** word explodes in your heart through faith, then your mouth must give testimony to it. And, the most powerful form that your mouth can give testimony through, is in the action of New Testament praise to the Lord. ***This is the key then for how praise releases faith.***

8

The New Birth

Ye Must Be Born Again

One day, a rich, young ruler came to Jesus and said, "...Good Master, what good thing shall I do, that I may have eternal life?" (Matt. 19:16).

There are two points about his question that I want you to notice. First of all, the young man was aware of the fact that he needed eternal life. Secondly, he thought he had to **do** something good in order to get it.

Why do you think he asked the question? What did he recognize to be missing inside of himself? He obviously figured that Jesus had an answer for him, because he came to Jesus with the question. He was looking to Jesus to solve this problem for him.

There is something of that young man in all of us. All of us—in fact, every man and woman born on the face of the earth—must ask themselves that all-important question: What must I do to have eternal life? There is a hunger deep within, something that is unsatisfied, a craving on the inside of man that feels the need for something more. Notice the young man knew it had something to do with the word "life."

There is a certain deadness inside a person. Man's human spirit is dead, and yearning for life. I believe the spirit has continued to exist in man right from the day when Adam sinned, but our spirits are void of the ability to communicate with God or to be the recipients of God's communication to us. So, in a very real sense, our spirits are dead because they aren't working the way they were intended to work.

The great French philosopher and theologian, Pascal, called this spiritual void in man a *"God-shaped vacuum, which only Christ could fill."* Even though the human spirit is void of any spiritual life in the one who has not been born again, its very inactive presence in the unbeliever still plays an important role. It serves as a constant reminder that something very basic is missing from our inner beings. Augustine once said, *"You have made us for yourself, O God, and our hearts are restless until they find their rest in you."*

People will search in many areas to fulfill this sense of something missing. This accounts for the many people who give themselves to the worldly pursuits of sex, money, fame, power, beauty, pleasure, and religion. These forces however cannot satisfy or fill the inner void in the spirit which only Christ can fill.

One of the best illustrations concerning man's need to be born again is found in a conversation Jesus had with a leading religious teacher of Israel, Nicodemus. The story is found in John 3. He was a sincere and godly man, which is indicated by the fact that he came looking for Jesus and searching for truth. In their conversation, Jesus revealed one of the great truths of the Kingdom of God. He said that man must have a spiritual rebirth in order to comprehend God and His Kingdom. Jesus made a statement that applies to every one of us: "Except a man be born again, he cannot see the kingdom of God" (John 3:3)

An obvious question arises for us at this point:

How is a man born again? In 1 Peter 1:23, the Bible says, "Being born again, not of corruptible seed, but of incorruptible, *by the word of God,* which liveth and abideth forever" (italics mine). Peter tells us that a man is born again by the incorruptible seed of the Word of God. In other words, the Word of God creates the new birth in a believer's life.

Another Effect of God's Word—
The New Birth

In the last chapter we were discussing the effects that God's Word produces in a believer's life. We said in the last chapter that the Word produces faith. *Now we are going to see that the new birth is also created by the Word of God.*

There is life in the Word, a divine energy, a surging, powerful force that automatically creates new life or the new birth in a believer's heart. Someone who does not know Jesus and who is an unbeliever can spend time in the Word of God, and if he is willing to believe that Word, it will create eternal life in his heart. A miracle will take place. Why? Because the Word has that life-giving power within it; it creates the new birth.

I would like to take a much closer look at the term "born again" or "the new birth." In understanding the working of the Word of God, it is vital for us to see how it creates new life in a believer's heart. In order to understand the new birth, it is necessary for us to understand the nature of man.

In this regard, let us take a look at 1 Thessalonians 5:23. The Scripture says, "And the very God of peace sanctify you wholly; and I pray God your whole spirit and soul and body be preserved blameless unto the coming of our Lord Jesus Christ." In this verse, Paul declares that a believer's personality has three parts to it—*spirit, soul, and body.* You are a spirit, you have a soul, and you live in a body.

Your spirit is God-conscious, your soul is self-conscious, your body is sense-conscious or world-conscious.

The writer of Hebrews mentions the fact that, "...the word of God is quick, and powerful, and sharper than any twoedged sword, piercing even to the dividing asunder of soul and spirit..." (Heb. 4:12). Obviously, the soul and spirit are hard to separate. How do you tell the difference between them? The writer says that the Word of God is like a sword; it will divide and separate between soul and spirit, and it will show us the contrasts.

In God's Image

Let us look for a moment, at what the Word of God has to say about man as spirit, soul, and body. To understand this subject properly, I want to go back to Genesis 1:26. The Bible says, "And God said, Let us make man in our image, after our likeness: and let them have dominion over the fish of the sea, and over the fowl of the air, and over the cattle, and over all the earth, and over every creeping thing that creepeth upon the earth."

Notice the fact that God had a purpose in creating man. Man was created to rule. He was created to have dominion over fish, foul, cattle, and every creeping thing. **Man was to present the image of God to the rest of creation.** That's why God said these words, "Let us make man in our image, after our likeness."

The word "image" is very interesting in its original Hebrew. It is the word **"tselem."** In other passages, it is translated as "shadow." It is used in the modern Hebrew language and it now means to have your photograph taken.

What God is saying in these words is that man has been made after God's outward physical outline and form. **Did you know that God has a physical** *outline and form, and in our external form, we project the likeness and the image of God?* There are constant references in the Scriptures to the fact that God has hair, eyes, a nose, and feet. The Bible tells us that Jesus is at the right hand of the throne of God; He's not at the left hand.

It is so important that we understand God the way He is truly presented to us in the Scriptures. He is not some vague form or mysterious glory cloud; He does have outward physical outline and form, and this verse tells us that mankind is made in His image. That's why Jesus was incarnated as a man. *It was appropriate for the Son of God to appear among us as a man.*

When you realize you are made in the outward image of God, it affects the way you think about yourself. That image you see in the mirror when you get up in the morning, is formed after the image of Almighty God. The Bible says you are fearfully and wonderfully made.

Genesis 1:26 also points out that we are made after God's likeness. The word used here indicates an inward comparison, an inward likeness. Even as God is three persons, (He is a triune God—God the Father, God the Son, and God the Holy Spirit), man also is a triune being. Man is spirit, soul and body.

The First Creation

To understand how God made us as spirit, soul, and body we will examine Genesis 2:7. In this verse we see a description of the actual process of creation. This is a story of man being born the first time. Later on, I will make the comparison of man being born again (the second birth). "And the Lord God formed man of the dust of the ground, and breathed into his nostrils the breath of life; and man became a living soul" (Gen. 2:7). This verse introduces to us a new name for God.

Genesis 1, God is referred to as
the plural ending (**im**) and implies
a Trinity, Father, Son, and Holy Spirit.
ver, the name used here is a name so sacred
that even today the Jews will not pronounce it. The
translators of the King James Version refer to it as
Jehovah. In the Hebrew language, this word is composed of four consonants. The vowels in a name or in
a word are not written in Hebrew. So this word for
Jehovah has the four consonants Y H W H. An obvious question occurs: what vowels do you put between
the consonants? *No one knows the answers.*

Modern scholars have made the word read
Yahweh, which means *"He will be"* or *"He is what
He is."* This sacred name appears here in Genesis
2:7. It is a personal name for God. There is a reason
for God creating man, and that reason for creation is
fellowship.

Before we look more thoroughly at this verse, I
want to refer you to John 1:1-3:

**1 In the beginning was the Word, and the Word
was with God, and the Word was God.
2 The same was in the beginning with God.
3 All things were made by him; and without him
was not any thing made that was made.**

The Word Created All Things

Notice verse 3 of this text, *"All things were
made by him..."* Who does "him" refer to in this
verse? It refers back to verse 1, "In the beginning was
the Word..." "The Word" in this text refers to Jesus
Christ, the Son of God, and *it is obvious that Jesus
Christ made all things.*

Notice the next phrase, "...and without him was
not any thing made that was made." It is important
to understand in creation that all creation started
with God the Father, but that Jesus Himself was the

agent of creation. The Father initiated the creative process, but the actual creation itself proceeded through the Son. Jesus was actively involved in making all things. You cannot truly understand Genesis 2:7 without this insight.

In Genesis 2:7 we see that Jesus is directly involved in creating Adam. The Word, the eternal Word, is active here. Jesus, as the Word of God, is in the process of creating the first man. That is why the term *"Jehovah,"* speaking of God in His personal sense, is used in this context. In this reference, Jehovah refers directly to Jesus Christ.

"And the Lord God formed man of the dust of the ground..." The word "formed" is the Hebrew word *"yatsar,"* and it means "to mold into a form." It carries the idea of a potter forming clay. It also has within it a reference to something that is done with great care and precision. It seems to indicate that in the creative process, although God created all things, He took special care in forming man out of the dust of the ground. In other words, His attention is especially focused upon the creation of Adam.

Notice that man was formed out of the dust of the ground. It is obvious that there must have been some kind of moisture in that dust to make it adhere and take shape. A better word to use in this text would be "clay." Can you see the picture here? It is so powerful if your faith can grasp it. Jesus molds a body of clay on the ground, it is an absolutely perfect sculpture, better than anything man has ever tried to design or make. I see a picture in my mind's eye of that sculpture, that body of clay laying on its back, a lifeless form.

Then the verse says, "...the Lord...breathed into his nostrils the breath of life..." Jesus must have been kneeling beside the form of Adam on the ground. Can you see this? God stoops down to bring life into the clay. This is a divine picture of God's action toward man.

So here we see it, Jesus stooping over the clay, and putting His nostrils to the nostrils of the about-to-be Adam—lips on his lips, **and then He breathes.** Hallelujah! The divine breath, the breath of God, the Spirit of God, enters the clay and the clay becomes a living person.

What power we see manifested here. Adam comes alive with real hair, real eyes, an incredible nervous system; his heart begins to beat, the blood courses through the veins and arteries, the glands function, the tissues are perfectly formed, the hands, the fingers—*this is the story of the first creation.*

The Explosive, Creative Power of God

It seems so easy for God to do this, but the message for us is profound. *If He made us easily the first time, then He can heal us easily the second time.* The Holy Spirit who brought every function of your body into being can repair any part of your body. The explosive, creative power of God that brought Adam into perfect being—that same Holy Spirit—is in you now. Your body is His temple. The very breath of God is in you now. That Spirit is in you to bring you life. He can create or restore any part of your body. *It is very easy to believe in healing if you can see this picture.* Praise the Lord!

The next part of Genesis 2:7 says, "...and man became a living soul." Notice in this verse you have man in his triune being; all three parts are referred to in the verse. When God breathed His breath into man, man came alive spiritually. You have within you the eternal breath of God; you have a spirit. But notice, God breathed into the dust or the clay of the ground; it was the clay that became the body.

Notice also that the union of the breath of God and the molded clay brought into being a third part that is called the soul. Man became a living soul. So you have in this verse spirit, soul and body. The soul was automatically created when the spirit came in contact with the body, and in that sense, the soul is the point of contact between your spirit and your body.

The spirit is the part of man that is made after the image of God. It is that sense in us that yearns after God, it is always reaching up for God. But there is something else in us that pulls us down—our bodies—and they are prone to sin. The source of all conflict in man is found in this dichotomy.

The soul is the seat of man's will. Man makes individual decisions; will he allow his soul to be controlled by his spirit or by his body? When his spirit is in control, he is flowing toward God. When his body is in control, he is flowing toward the flesh. The soul makes the decision.

Perhaps the best way to understand the mystery of creation is to look at the very expressive Hebrew words that are used for spirit and soul.

The Hebrew word for spirit is *"ruach."* The last letter has a sound which doesn't exist in English. I heard it first on one of my missionary journeys to South Africa in the Afrikaanse language. you will also hear it in the accents of the Scottish people. We call it a soft, aspirated "h." When a Scotsman says "loch," he pronounces the 'ch' with a semi-gutteral sound. All Semitic languages have this sound. In order to pronounce it, you have to produce a steady, continuing, outgoing breath. When a Scotsman says "loch" he can continue on with the 'h' as long as he likes.

The Spirit of God is represented by God's breath. The Spirit is the continuing, outgoing breath of God. It continues on and on, and the word *"ruach"* represents that breath of God to us. It is the Spirit Himself Who initiates all life. Because He is life, He breathes life out to all mankind.

The word for soul in the Hebrew is the word *"nephesh."* Remember I mentioned that in Hebrew, you don't write the vowels. So in writing this word in Hebrew, you would write three different consonants—N, F and SH. In pronouncing these consonants, you have a sound that is very similar to sleeping. You inhale or breathe in with a pronunciation of the N, and then you expel with the pronunciation of the F and the SH. It sounds like a person in a deep sleep. If you say the word to yourself, you will immediately hear what I am referring to. Notice the order, however; *first you breathe in and then you breathe out.*

This is a true depiction of the human soul. The soul is dependent life. It must first breathe in the breath of God and then breathe out its own soulish life. *The soul must receive before it can give out.* The spirit originates and gives, the soul receives and then gives.

To sum up, we see Jesus kneeling over the form of Adam. He places nostrils to nostrils and lips to lips, and then in the power of the Holy Spirit, He breathes. It is a very powerful, outgoing breath. It carries with it the explosion of divine energy. God put everything into it. He breathes into Adam, and Adam came alive. This is a powerful picture of the first birth.

The Second Birth

What then is the second birth? What did Jesus mean when He said to Nicodemus, "...Ye must be born again"? (John 3:7).

Do you remember the story of the resurrection of Jesus as it is recorded in John 20? In the evening time, on the day of the resurrection, the disciples had gathered together because they were afraid of the Jews, and suddenly Jesus stood in the midst of them and said, "...Peace be unto you" (verse 21). He showed them His hands and His feet, and the Bible says the disciples were glad when they saw the Lord. Then Jesus said to them, "...as my Father hath sent me, even so send I you."

Notice specifically verse 22, "And when he had said this, he breathed on them, and saith unto them, Receive ye the Holy Ghost." When you remember the story of the first creation and see Jesus bending over Adam and breathing into him the breath of life, this story in John 20 takes on a brand-new significance. It is the same person, Jesus—the eternal Word of God.

The disciples have actually seen Him. They have been able to reach out and touch Him. Their faith has been ignited. They truly believe that Jesus is the Son of God, that He has been raised from the dead. After that process of believing, Jesus breathes on them.

Here is Jesus, through the energy of the life-giving spirit, transmitting the very energy and nature of God into the spirit of the disciples. At that very moment, the disciples were born again. They experienced the life of God. The miracle of the new birth took place. They were born again through the power of the living Word.

What Happened in Eden?

It is important for us to understand what happened in the Garden of Eden. When Adam and Eve were created, they were given a human spirit that enabled them to commune with God. Their spirits did not contain the uncreated eternal life of God, however. As long as they were in the Garden, they had God Himself there. And that was all they needed then. However, Satan came to the Garden and tempted them to sin. He said, "...hath God said?" He questioned the eternal Word of God.

Then Adam and Eve ate from the fruit of the tree of the knowledge of good and evil. They sinned, and as a consequence they lost their spiritual life and communion with God. From that moment to this, mankind's spirit has been dead. Perhaps a better word would be **non-functioning or dormant.** Man's spirit has been hungering after God.

In the new birth, however, man encounters life—the life of God. The Bible says, **"In him was life; and the life was the light of men."** (John 1:4). This, of course, is a reference to Jesus. "That was the true Light, which lighteth every man that cometh into the world" (John 1:9). Jesus called Himself "the light of the world."

"...he that followeth me shall not walk in darkness, but shall have the light of life" (John 8:12).

When a person is born again, he receives life, and in that life the light goes on inside of him. For the first time he is able to understand the things of God and the spiritual realm. That's why a believer understands the new birth. But to an unbeliever, it all sounds like foolishness.

The Life of God

The Greek word translated as "life" in this verse is **"zoe." Zoe** means the life of God. We use the term "eternal life." The Scriptures say, "For as the Father hath life in himself; so hath he given to the Son to have life in himself" (John 5:26).

Remember the truth of John 1:4, "In him was life; and the life was the light of men." When we receive that life of God, He is actually imparting His very nature and being to our human spirits. In the new birth, our spirits are born of God. "Therefore if any man be in Christ, he is a new creature: old things are passed away; behold, all things are become new" (2 Cor. 5:17). It is the life and nature of God coming into your spirit that makes you a new creation. It makes your inward man a new man.

If you are a believer, it is absolutely vital for you to recognize that this life is inside of you. That life is bringing you light. It is absolutely vital for you to declare every day: "His life is in me; the life of God is in me. I've got God in me. I've got God's wisdom in me. I've got God's life in me. I've got God's power in me. Praise the Lord!" Only when you see it and believe it will you give expression to the explosive power of that life.

Remember the words of Paul in 1 Corinthians 6:19, "What? know ye not that your body is the temple of the Holy Ghost which is in you, which ye have of God, and ye are not your own?" Praise God; that life is alive inside of you. That life is there to heal you now. That life is there to bless you financially right now. That life is there to transform your relationships right now. You are in vital union with God Himself. God has moved out of an earth-made, man-made holy of holies; He dwells in you. You are the temple where the holy shekinah presence of God dwells.

Is This Life Inside of Me?

An obvious question arises in many minds at this point: "How can I know that what you are saying is true? How do I know that there really is life inside of me? I wasn't in the upper room with the disciples. Jesus didn't breathe on me and say, 'Receive the Holy Spirit.' I've never even seen Jesus. How do I know that His life is inside of me?"

How does God's Word work? In the last chapter we said that the Word creates faith. In this chapter, we are declaring that **the Word creates the new birth.** You may ask, "Which Word are you talking about? Are you talking about Jesus Christ, the living Word of God, or are you talking about the Scriptures, the written Word of God?" They both contain the divine nature of God. Jesus is not present in physical form in your house right now, but His Word brings His presence to you in written form. The written Word does everything that the living Word of Jesus did when He was on the earth. *The written Word brings to you the very life of God Himself.*

Let me illustrate what I am trying to say by taking you back again to the story of Mary in Luke 1:26-37. The angel Gabriel had been sent from God into a city called Nazareth to a virgin whose name was Mary. The angel saluted Mary and said, "...Hail, thou that art highly favoured, the Lord is with thee: blessed art thou among women" (verse 28).

Mary was disturbed by what the angel said. But the angel went on, "...behold, thou shalt conceive in thy womb, and bring forth a son, and shalt call his name JESUS" (verse 31). Mary asked an obvious question, "...How shall this be, seeing I know not a man?" (verse 34). The angel answered her with the most powerful words: "For with God nothing shall be impossible" (verse 37).

Remember what I mentioned in a previous chapter, the word "nothing" in the Greek is composed of two words—*"no rhema."* In effect, the angel is saying, "For with God no **rhema** or 'no word that God speaks' shall be impossible." Another translation has it as follows: "No Word of God shall be void of power." Here we have a double negative. If you were to put it in the positive, it would be translated this way: *"Every word that God speaks contains the power for its own fulfillment."*

Try to catch a picture of what is happening here. God has summoned the angel Gabriel to His throne. He says, "Gabriel, take my Word to a young woman in Nazareth." The angel carries the Word of God out of heaven, down to earth. He brings that Word to the young woman. She finds it hard to believe. In order to convince her, the angel says, "Mary, the very word

I am speaking to you now contains the power in it for its own fulfillment." Mary had to make a decision. Would she believe or not believe? Her response to the angel is classic. She said, "...be it unto me according to thy word" (Luke 1:38). Her faith hooked up with the words of the angel.

She had just heard the angel tell her that God's Word contained within it the power to make her pregnant. She believed what the angel said, and I believe that she was instantly made pregnant. God's Word made her pregnant. Can you see this? The spoken Word was carried from God out of heaven, believed on by a young woman, and her faith transformed that spoken Word into a living person in her womb. The spoken Word out of heaven became the living Word, Jesus Christ, in Mary's womb. Pause and think about that.

There was life in the Word. There was creative energy to bring God's Son into the womb of Mary. Only when you see the power of that spoken and written Word will your faith come alive for the kinds of miracles God wants His Word to produce in your life.

It's the Same Today

When I preach in a great gospel crusade service, the same thing happens. I am a messenger of God. I put His words on my lips. I open my heart to flow under the anointing of the Holy Spirit. If there is someone in my audience who is an unbeliever, as they listen to the Word of God which I preach, they must make a decision: Will they be like Mary? Will they say, "Be it unto me according to thy Word?"

The angel had told Mary that the Word contained the power for its own fulfillment, and I believe this when I preach to an audience. The Word that I preach will save their souls, if they will believe. And so I encourage any man, woman, or young person to believe on the message of that Word. If they believe, something happens.

The Word of God under the anointing is transformed by their faith into a living Jesus Who comes alive in their hearts. The written Word that is breathed on by the power of the Holy Spirit, becomes the living Savior to their hearts. *That is why it is such an honor to be a preacher of the gospel.* That is why it is such a solemn responsibility and opportunity to be able to bring that kind of life to people.

The same principle holds true in the area of healing. The healing power of God is alive in my mouth as I declare it to the multitudes. When we come to a time of praise and worship in our crusade services, I encourage people to raise their hands and open their hearts to God. Then the healing power of God that has been unleashed through the preaching of the Word and under the anointing begins to make sick bodies whole.

The same Jesus who bent over Adam and breathed life into him through the power of the Holy Spirit begins to breathe on the human bodies of people in the audience and the signs and the wonders and the miracles of God are manifested among us. You must see the key here. I preach from the written Word. That written Word comes alive under the anointing. That same anointing is on the words of this book. They will come alive to you now if you will believe.

I remember a tremendous healing that took place in 1986. I had been invited to speak for the General Council of the Assemblies of God in Great Britain. There were approximately 6,000 people attending the conference. There was a strong flow of praise and worship in the meetings.

In my healing service I encouraged everyone to

raise their hands in praise. I watched a dignified lady on the front row. She was a school teacher about fifty-five years of age. She had Parkinson's disease and had lost mobility in the upper right side of her body. She could not control her right hand. It would bump into the people beside her. But I could see faith written on her face.

She was determined to get her right hand into the air in order to praise the Lord. Then I saw it happen. The power of the Lord touched her hand. At first she was surprised; then she was overjoyed. She came up on the platform beside me. She held her hand out and moved her fingers.

"I haven't been able to do this for four years," she said. There were about fifteen pastors behind me on the platform. They were deeply moved. My England office has been in touch with her recently. There is not one vestige of Parkinson's Disease in her body. The same Jesus who breathed life into Adam created healing in that body. Praise the Lord!

9

The Word of God Heals

Physical Health and Strength

We have been discussing the effects of the Word of God. The first effect that God's Word produces in the life of the believer is faith. The second effect produced by the Word of God is the new birth. **The third working of the Word of God is healing,** and this is the topic for this chapter.

It is an amazing fact to me that God's Word is so varied and wonderful in the way it works. It not only provides faith and the new birth, but it also provides physical health and strength for the human body.

One of the most powerful Scriptures regarding this is found in Psalms 107:17-20 (italics are mine):

17 Fools because of their transgression, and because of their iniquities, are afflicted.
18 Their soul abhorreth all manner of meat; and they draw near unto the gates of death.
19 Then they cry unto the Lord in their trouble, and he saveth them out of their distresses.
20 *He sent his word, and healed them, and delivered them from their destructions.*

The picture the Psalmist gives us here is a sad one indeed. He is describing men who appear to be almost dead. Their bodies are sick; they have even lost their appetite for food. In the midst of their trouble, they cry out to the Lord for healing. How does God answer their prayer? He answers it by sending His Word and healing them and delivering them from their destructions. It is obvious from this verse, therefore, *that both healing and deliverance come to us through God's Word.*

In the last chapter we discussed the power of **zoe**—the energy of the eternal life that flows in the Word. That very **zoe** (or life) creates the new birth in a believer's life. That same **zoe** (or life) also creates healing power in the physical body, and the Psalmist is trying to impress these facts on our hearts in Psalm 107:20.

Isaiah says something very important in this regard: "So shall my word be that goeth forth out of my mouth: it shall not return unto me void, but it shall accomplish that which I please, *and it shall prosper in the thing whereto I sent it"* (Isa. 55:11, italics mine).

The Psalmist says that God sent His Word to heal and to deliver (see Ps. 107:20). Then in Isaiah we read that God says His Word shall prosper in the thing whereto He sent it. (see Isa. 55:11). This means one simple thing: *if God sent His word to heal, then it is going to heal.* There is no question about it. Case dismissed. His Word will prosper in the thing whereunto it has been sent. This is an unequivocal fact. The healing power is resident in God's Word, and God has sent that Word to heal the sick. This fact should encourage great faith in the hearts of those who come to receive the Word of God.

If God's Word heals, the next important question to ask is, what does it heal? What is healing? Healing is a complex subject in the Scriptures, and should not be approached in a simplistic way. *There are many different kinds of healing mentioned in the Word of God.* In fact, the word "healing" itself is often the same Greek word *"sozo"* that is used for salvation, which basically means to be saved from the devil's power and restored in the wholeness of God's order and well-being by the power of God's Spirit.

It is important for us to ask what kind of healing we can expect from the Word of God. I have tried to emphasize over and over again the fact that Jesus is the living Word and the Scriptures are the written Word. In essence, they are one and the same. They both bring to us the divine *"zoe"* or the divine nature or life of Almighty God Himself. I believe the healing referred to in Psalms 107:20, "He sent his word, and healed them..." refers to healing in a general sense (in other words, all kinds of healing).

Different Kinds of Healing

There are several different kinds of healing found in the Scriptures. The first is healing of the human body. It involves the restoration of the original physical condition so that the body functions properly. Jesus demonstrated this type of healing when he spoke a word on behalf of the centurion's servant who was sick with paralysis.

The next kind is the healing of the demonized. In Matthew 12 Jesus healed a blind and dumb man whose illness was attributed to demonization. In Luke 13 he healed a woman bound by an evil spirit *causing curvature of the spine for eighteen years.*

A third kind of healing is healing of the spirit, or salvation. Jesus said to the man let down through the roof, "Son, thy sins be forgiven thee." The physical sickness was healed as a direct result of the healing of the spiritual sickness.

Another kind of healing is the raising of the dead. This kind of healing, perhaps more than any other, manifests the dramatic ability of the Word of God to invade Satan's final stronghold—death. Jesus raised Jairus's daughter with a command.

The healing of memories is another type of New Testament healing. We would call it inner healing. Jesus ministered emotional healing to Peter after he denied him three times. A few days after the resurrection, he found him fishing and asked him three times, "Do you love me? Then feed my sheep." This had to constitute a tremendous inner healing for Peter.

In all of these New Testament examples concerning healing, I am convinced of the fact that the New Testament Scriptures regard healing as affecting man as a whole. There is an integration of spirit, soul, and body in the healing manifestation of Jesus. Man is a total person, and if he is going to be healed, that healing must manifest itself in all areas of his person. You can be sick in one area of your physical being, but it automatically affects you in other areas as well. It is necessary for us, therefore, to approach the subject of healing *in a holistic manner.*

Where Does Sickness Come From?

There is one question that should be dealt with in this chapter, because it appears very often in the minds of many people. Where does sickness come from? Our answer is found in Romans 5:12: "Wherefore, as by one man sin entered into the world, and death by sin; and so death passed upon all men, for that all have sinned...." Physical death and all that it produces are the direct results of sin.

A quick reading of the early chapters of Genesis will indicate that it was Satan who caused our first parents to disobey God. So Satan is the real cause of sin, sickness, and death. It was Satan who caused Adam and Eve to disobey God's command, so Satan is the real author of sickness. Sickness is a result of sin.

This explains why Jesus said to the man whom He cured at the pool of Bethesda in John 5:14, "...sin no more, lest a worse thing come unto thee." His sickness had come on him as a result of his sin.

It is interesting in the New Testament to notice how Jesus rebuked sickness. The word *"epitimao"* is used often. It is a harsh word, often used by Jesus in rebuking evil spirits. In other words, He rebuked sickness in the same way He rebuked evil spirits.

In Luke 4:35 we read, "And Jesus rebuked him, saying, Hold thy peace, and come out of him...." Jesus is dealing with a demon here. Four verses later in Luke 4:39, Jesus stood over Simon Peter's mother-in-law and rebuked (the same *epitimesen)* the fever that was in her.

In Jesus' understanding, it is obvious that both sickness and evil spirits were caused by Satan, and *so He rebuked them.* Acts 10:38 says, "How God anointed Jesus of Nazareth with the Holy Ghost and with power: who went about doing good, and *healing all that were oppressed of the devil;* for God was with him" (italics mine).

The Greek word used for "oppressed" in this verse really means those under domination or attack of Satan. Not only is Satan the originator of sickness, but he is the propagator of it as well.

In Luke 13:11 we have the story of the woman who had a spirit of infirmity eighteen years and was bowed together and could in no wise lift herself up. In verse 16 of that chapter, we are informed that this was Satan's work: "And ought not this woman, being a daughter of Abraham, whom Satan hath bound, lo, these eighteen years, be loosed from this bond on the sabbath day?" This woman was sick with the spirit of infirmity that actually caused curvature of the spine. *There are some spirits that cause physical sickness.*

Healing From Evil Spirits

Some time ago, I was invited by the International Lutheran Conference on the Holy Spirit to preach at their meeting in Minneapolis. They asked me to conduct a healing service. First, I preached the Word and then I prayed for the sick. There were about 6,000 present in the auditorium. The healing power of God moved amongst the people, and I asked those who had experienced a physical touch from the Lord to come forward. Somewhere between 300 and 400 people moved toward the front.

Because of the lateness of the hour, we had very little opportunity to hear many of the healing testimonies. However, I was invited to continue our meeting in Minneapolis at North Heights Lutheran Church the following week.

That week a man came into my service at North Heights, and told me an unusual story. He had been in our healing service six days before in the Minneapolis auditorium. He had a precancerous condition in his prostate. He had been that way for ten years. He had lived in constant and excruciating pain. He had taken antibiotics for ten years.

He said, "Terry, when you commanded healing in the lower tract of the body and specifically mentioned prostate, the burning sensation I had had in my prostate for ten years *jumped out of the prostate and into my thighs.* It scared me because I didn't know what was happening. Then you went on to pray for other areas of the body, and the burning sensation moved out of my thighs, down through my legs, and finally out of my feet. It was the first time in ten years that the pain and the burning had left me, and I felt that I was healed."

He went to his personal physician immediately. The physician examined him and said, "I find no trace of disease in your body. Your prostate appears to be entirely healed.

How he rejoiced as he told me the story of his healing that night. I knew immediately, as he mentioned the symptoms of his healing, that he had been afflicted by an evil spirit. That burning sensation responded to the command of God's Word that came from my lips.

The spirit who was afflicting him heard me speak and left the area of the prostate when I commanded it to leave. However, it did not want to leave the body completely. When I continued to command in other areas of the body, it ultimately left the body, and the man was made whole.

Satan has all kinds of evil spirits. Some of these spirits attack the minds of people and cause mental illness. Others of them are designated as spirits of sickness, and they come against the human body.

Our conclusion is simple. Satan is not only the originator of sickness and disease, but he manifests both by means of evil spirits. This does not mean, however, that all disease directly involves an evil spirit.

I have always been interested in the way evil spirits respond to the Word of God. Several years ago, I had an opportunity to conduct a healing crusade in the state of Florida. One night, a particularly strong anointing came on me as I was preaching concerning the power of God's Word to heal the sick. In the service, a lady leaned over to her husband and said, "Why do I resent that man so much when he preaches on the power of God's Word?" Her husband did not have an answer, and said, "Let's talk about this when we get home."

The woman had been a charismatic believer for fifteen years. When they got home, the husband agreed to pray for his wife and placed his hand on her head to do so. As soon as he did, an evil spirit spoke out and said, "What Terry Law says about the Word of God is not correct. The Word does not have that kind of power."

The man was shocked to hear his wife say this. He immediately went to the telephone and called me, asking what he should do. I encouraged him by telling him not to be concerned, but rather to bring her over to where I was. When he did, I dealt with the spirit and it left immediately.

It was a powerful reminder to me of the battle that goes on between the Kingdom of God and the kingdom of darkness. Our weapon in that battle is the Word of God. When we speak it, when we preach it, when we declare it, we come into direct conflict with the enemy himself. **But the Word of God has power to heal.** Praise the Lord!

The Children's Bread

In Matthew 15:21-28, we have the story of the Syrophonecian woman. She had a daughter who was seriously troubled by an evil spirit. She came to Jesus, but Jesus answered her not a word. His disciples were upset with the woman and wanted Him to send her away. The woman cried out, "Lord, help me." But Jesus answered, "...It is not meet to take *the children's bread,* and to cast it to dogs" (verse 26, italics mine). By these words, Jesus indicated that healing is the *children's bread.*

In other words, healing is a part of God's appointed, daily provision for all His children. If you are a child of God, then you have a direct right to receive it. Notice that Jesus called it "bread." Bread is a staple part of our diets. It is a daily provision for us from the Father. We shouldn't have to make special requests in order to receive the healing. *It belongs to us; it is the children's bread.*

Let us look at Proverbs 4:20-22 in this regard (italics are mine):

20 My son, attend to my words; incline thine ear unto my sayings.
21 Let them not depart from thine eyes; keep them in the midst of thine heart.
22 *For they are life unto those that find them, and health to all their flesh.*

The writer here makes a direct connection between the Word of God and healing. He says His words are life and health unto those who find them. The word "find" is significant in this context. When you find something, you take possession of it.

The Word of God is the same. Just because you've memorized a Scripture verse doesn't mean you've found it. It doesn't mean you've received the revelation of the inner meaning of those words. You must find what that inner meaning is. **You must catch the rhema revelation of God.** When you do, those words will be life unto you and they will become health to all your flesh.

Oh, how important it is that we catch the power of God's Word. Hebrews 11:3 says, "Through faith we understand that the worlds were framed by the word of God, so that things which are seen were not made of things which do appear." When we, as children of the living God, begin to realize the creative power that is contained in what God says, when He speaks, we will immediately begin to believe for the impossible. Until we learn the power of God's Word, that Word has not yet become a living thing to us.

Is the Word, the Scripture, a living thing to you? It is not just a book of beautiful doctrines or creeds or dogmas; it is not just the product of a printer or a combination of paper and ink. Listen to what Jesus says, "...the words that I speak unto you, *they are spirit, and they are life."* (John 6:63)

When God speaks through His Word, the same creative power that was drawn upon when He spoke the world into existence goes into action again. His Word today is just as effective, just as powerful, just as creative as it was when the worlds were framed by the Word of God.

Ezekiel 12:25 says, "For I am the Lord: I will speak, and the word that I shall speak shall come to pass...." Matthew 24:35, "Heaven and earth shall pass away, but my words shall not pass away." 1 Peter 1:25, "But the word of the Lord endureth for ever." Romans 4:21, "...what he had promised, he was able also to perform." Luke 1:37, "No word from God is void of power or ability" (my paraphrase).

He is a Healing God

God says in Exodus 15:26: "...for I am the Lord that healeth thee." If you dare to believe the power of those wonderful words, then those words will come alive in you. Act on them now. Get off your bed of sickness; your faith will make you whole. The lame man will begin to leap like a deer, the tongue of the dumb will begin to sing, deaf ears will open, pains will flee, darkness will be banished. You will be healed by the creative power of God's Word.

The creative power of God's Word will create the very thing in your body that you need in order to be well and strong. Weakness will be transformed into strength, death will be transformed into life, sickness will be transformed into health. If God could create the entire world with His words, "let there be," then surely He can heal your sick body with His Word.

The word of a man is what a man is. **The Word is what God is.** Unbelief in this Word is unbelief in God Who is the Author of it. Our attitude toward this Word of God means everything. The first thing that amazed the people of Jesus' day and caught their attention was the fact that Jesus spoke with such power and authority.

In Luke 4:32, the Scripture says, "And they were astonished at his doctrine...." Why? "...for his word was with power." And they exclaimed, "...What a word is this! for with authority and power he commandeth the unclean spirits, and they come out" (verse 36).

I say the same thing to you: this Word is with power; there is authority in the Word. *This Word comes to heal you now.*

Let Down Your Net

Remember the story in Luke 5 when Jesus came to the fishermen in the early morning? They had been laboring all night with their fishing nets, trying to catch a few fish in order to make an honest living, but they had caught nothing. In verses 4 and 5 we read how Jesus came and said:

> **4 ...Launch out into the deep, and let down your nets for a draught.**
> **5 And Simon answering said unto him, Master, we have toiled all the night, and have taken nothing: nevertheless at thy word I will let down the net.**

Now notice those words, *"...nevertheless at thy word I will let down the net."*

Friend, the Word of the Lord comes to you now, *it's time to let down your net.* Peter did not stop to argue. He didn't say to Jesus, "The case is hopeless, it won't work." He didn't say that there were no fish in those waters, even though he had been searching for them all night long.

Friend, the thoughts of the enemy may rise up in your heart at this very moment and say, "But the doctors say this and the specialists say that; I've gone to this man for healing; I've gone to that man for healing; I've been prayed for by everyone." Forget all of your excuses and react like Peter. Say what he did.

"Nevertheless at thy word I will let down my net."

Give yourself in full obedience to this Word of God. Remember, there is no Word from God that is void of power. He will fill your net if you will let it down right now. Say it in your heart, "Nevertheless, at thy Word I will believe, at thy Word I will be healed, at thy Word I will be delivered. I receive Your healing Word now. Thank you, Jesus."

Scripture Verses That Heal

Isaiah 53:5-6:

5 But he was wounded for our transgressions, he was bruised for our iniquities: the chastisement of our peace was upon him; and with his stripes we are healed.
6 All we like sheep have gone astray; we have turned every one to his own way; and the Lord hath laid on him the iniquity of us all.

Matthew 8:16-17:

16 When the even was come, they brought unto him many that were possessed with devils: and he cast out the spirits with his word, and healed all that were sick:
17 That it might be fulfilled which was spoken by Esaias the prophet, saying, Himself took our infirmities, and bare our sicknesses.

1 Peter 2:24, "Who his own self bare our sins in his own body on the tree, that we, being dead to sins, should live unto righteousness: by whose stripes ye were healed."

Luke 10:19, "Behold, I give unto you power to tread on serpents and scorpions, and over all the power of the enemy: and nothing shall by any means hurt you."

Mark 16:15-18:

15 And he said unto them, Go ye into all the world, and preach the gospel to every creature.
16 He that believeth and is baptized shall be saved; but he that believeth not shall be damned.
17 And these signs shall follow them that believe; In my name shall they cast out devils; they shall speak with new tongues;
18 They shall take up serpents; and if they drink any deadly thing, it shall not hurt them; they shall lay hands on the sick, and they shall recover.

Exodus 15:26, "...for I am the Lord that healeth thee."

10

Abundance and Blessing

Blessings Overtake Us

We have been examining the effects produced by God's Word in the life of the believer. There is energy and life in the Word of God. In the last several chapters I have been outlining how that Word works. What effects does it produce?

The first effect God's Word produces is *faith.* The second effect is *the new birth.* The third effect is *healing.* In this chapter, I want to discuss the fourth working of the Word of God—*abundance and blessing.*

The Bible says in Deuteronomy 28:1, 2:

1 And it shall come to pass, if thou shalt hearken diligently unto the voice of the Lord thy God, to observe and to do all his commandments which I command thee this day, that the Lord thy God will set thee on high above all nations of the earth:
2 And all these blessings shall come on thee, and overtake thee....

The key phrase to notice is in verse 1: "If thou shalt hearken...to observe and to do all his commandments which I command thee this day...." Notice there is a direct connection between doing the Word of God and experiencing the blessings of God. In fact,

Moses says if we do God's Word, not only will we be blessed, but the blessings shall come on us and literally overtake us.

It is important for us to define our terms in this area so there will not be any misunderstanding.

Four primary words are used to speak of the blessings of God: riches, wealth, prosperity and abundance. When we think of riches and wealth, we think of having a great deal of money in the bank, or numerous material possessions.

In this chapter we will not focus so much on riches and wealth as on the use of the word "abundance." Let me give a definition of what I understand abundance to be. Abundance means you have everything you need and more left over so you can give to the needs of others. In other words, there is no lack in abundance; you always have more than you need.

It is my conviction that the Bible teaches that abundance is a direct result of the working of the Word of God. The world may not classify abundant people as being rich. Jesus would not have been classified as being rich, but He did have an abundance. All of His needs were met when they needed to be met. Abundance means not living in frustration or want. Abundance means the absence of want, need or lack. Prosperity is another word that can be used for abundance of this kind.

Is Abundance Good or Bad?

One basic question must be answered before we proceed further with the study of abundance: *Are abundance and prosperity good or bad?* If they are good, are they absolutely good? You will never come to a true Biblical faith in the area of abundance until you make up your mind about this question.

When a preacher discusses the question of

money, it often stirs up guilt in the hearts of the hearers. We have grown up over the years with a tremendous amount of emotion tied into the subject of money. **We feel guilty if we have lots of money and we feel guilty if we hardly have any money at all.** That is why the subject of money, in connection with the Kingdom of God, is so controversial. Most of us have seen fund-raising techniques that we regard as wrong. There has been much misuse and emotional manipulation in the area of fund-raising.

Much of our religious tradition tells us that wealth is bad. This is particularly true in Europe. It is commonly understood in Europe that if you are a minister of the gospel, you really shouldn't have very much abundance at all. They live with the idea that if you are going to be a Christian, you have to be miserable. Much of it has grown up around church tradition based on the monasticism of the Middle Ages.

I will never forget my first journey behind the Iron Curtain, into the Soviet Union. It was 1978 and I traveled there with one of our Living Sound teams to Leningrad and other Soviet cities. It was my first opportunity to meet with members of the underground church. I saw a commitment in their lives I had never seen before. In many ways, I was ashamed of the fact that I had never had to suffer for my faith in God.

I saw believers who had been beaten by the Soviet secret police. I saw believers who were living with practically nothing in order to see the advancement of the gospel of Jesus Christ. It affected me very deeply. It took me three or four weeks after I left the Soviet Union to get back to normal. Every time I thought about Russia I was stirred deeply and emotionally.

The first thing I did when I arrived home from the Soviet Union was to sell my car, buy a much cheaper one and give the excess money to use for believers in the Soviet Union. That was my first reaction. I felt guilty that I had something when they had nothing. Even though what I had was not that much in comparison to most North Americans, I felt guilty when I realized I had more than they did.

So again we come back to the fundamental question: Is abundance good or bad? There is no question that the teaching of the Scriptures, in both Old Testament and New Testament, is that prosperity and abundance are essentially good. In fact, they are absolutely good. Let me point out some Scriptures for your consideration.

What Does Scripture Say?

In Revelation 5, John, the beloved, is describing a vision of heaven. He describes the voices of many angels around the throne and the beasts and the elders; the numbers of them being ten thousand times ten thousand. In verse 12 he says, "Saying with a loud voice, Worthy is the Lamb that was slain to receive power, *and riches,* and wisdom, and strength, and honour, and glory and *blessing*." In the seven things that are ascribed to the Lamb, *riches* and *blessing* have an integral place. A close look at this verse shows us that riches are in very good company. If riches are to be regarded as God's favor bestowed on Jesus then who are we to make them evil here on the earth?

There is no question that many people have abused riches, but that doesn't make riches evil. Just because someone abuses something, doesn't mean it is necessarily bad. It would be bad, of course, if we abused it as others have. There is no question that many people have difficulty in handling riches and, consequently, there is a great danger in it. But that does not make riches innately evil.

In 1 Timothy 6:9, 10 Paul writes:

9 But they that will be rich fall into temptation

and a snare, and into many foolish and hurtful lusts, which drown men in destruction and perdition.
10 For the *love of money* is the root of all evil: which while some coveted after, they have erred from the faith, and pierced themselves through with many sorrows (italics mine).

A quick reading of these verses would indicate to some that money is evil and riches are wrong. But that is not what Paul is saying. Notice that *it is the love of money that is the root of all evil.* I know some people who are obsessed with the love of money and they hardly have a dime. You can covet money and not have any of it. It is not the money that is evil, it is the coveting that is wrong.

The next verse I want to look at is found in 1 Chronicles 29. David is offering a prayer of thanksgiving unto the Lord. In verses 11 and 12 he says:

11 Thine, O Lord, is the greatness, and the power, and the glory, and the victory, and the majesty: for all that is in the heaven and in the earth is thine; thine is the kingdom, O Lord, and thou art exalted as head above all.
12 Both riches and honour come of thee, and thou reignest over all; and in thine hand is power and might; and in thine hand it is to make great, and to give strength unto all.

Notice the declaration David makes in these verses; he says both riches and honor come from God. God is the ultimate source of riches. *If you regard riches as being evil, then you regard God as being evil,* because riches come from God and God cannot be tainted by evil. It is very important to set yourself straight in this regard.

Again in Deuteronomy 8, Moses instructs the children of Israel to remember the Lord. He is concerned that later on in life, when they have been blessed of God, they will forget the Lord. He says, "And thou say in thine heart, My power and the might of mine hand hath gotten me this wealth" (Deut. 8:17).

He goes on, "But thou shalt remember the Lord thy God: *for it is he that giveth thee power to get wealth,* that he may establish his covenant which he sware unto thy fathers, as it is this day" (Deut. 8:18, italics mine).

Who gives us the power to get wealth? **God.** There is no question that many people misuse the power given to them, but that does not make the wealth evil in and of itself. Why does God give wealth to His people? He does it to establish His covenant with them. Wealth is a manifestation of the fact that God is in covenant relationship with His children. You can see, through a close examination of the Word of God, that wealth and abundance are clearly attributed to being from God.

Why Does God Want My Money?

Someone always asks, *"But why does God want my money?"* The answer is really very simple. God doesn't want or need your money; God wants and needs *you.* And in receiving your money, He receives you. There is a key in this that is vitally important.

Your money represents what you spend forty hours a week earning on the job. When you take that money and spend it only on yourself, you are taking the benefits of the talent, the ability, the energy God gave you and you are using it selfishly. There is no indication at all that you are thankful to God for giving you the ability to make that money. God really doesn't have you until He has your money, because *when you give a portion of what you have received back to Him, you are declaring His Lordship in your life.*

Actually, a person's money reflects his spiritual health. I don't believe it is possible for a man to say that Jesus is Lord in his life if Jesus is not Lord of his pocketbook. I can tell more about your spirituality by a five-minute look at the balance sheet of your checkbook than I can by watching the way you live for a week. The way you spend your money shows your priorities in the Kingdom of God. That is why this subject of abundance stirs up such animated feelings in the Body of Christ.

Jesus talked a great deal about money. Sixteen of the thirty-eight parables of Christ deal with money and possessions and how to handle them. Jesus said more about money than He ever said about heaven and hell combined. In the gospels, one out of every ten verses deals with the subject of money—288 verses all together.

In the Bible there are five hundred verses on prayer, less than five hundred verses on faith, and over two thousand verses that deal with money and possessions. Why does this subject occupy such a major part of divine revelation? Obviously, God knew it would be a challenge. God knew people would get sidetracked in this area more than any other, and so He gave us very detailed instructions concerning how we are to handle our money.

Spiritual warfare is more evident in the area of money than it is anywhere else in our lives. Every year in the United States thousands of marriages break up over the subject of money. Satan has done everything he can to try to keep us from the truth in this area, but I believe with all of my heart that God has instructions for us in His Word that will lead us into blessing and abundance. Obedience to God's Word brings prosperity and abundance. Say that phrase over and over to yourself while you are reading this chapter: **Obedience to God's Word brings me prosperity and abundance.**

Blessing and Cursing

Deuteronomy 28 is called the chapter of blessing and cursing. Verses 2 to 13 speak of the blessings of God; *fruitfulness, abundance, protection, direction, victory, success, holiness, honor, riches,* and *dominion.* The curses are pronounced from verses 16 through 68. The curses include unfruitfulness, insufficiency, frustration, failure, defeat, bondage, *poverty,* fear, and every form of sickness, both mental and physical.

"And it shall come to pass, if thou shalt hearken diligently unto the voice of the Lord thy God, *to observe and to do all his commandments* which I command thee this day..." (Deut. 28:1, italics mine).

Notice, you hear the voice of the Lord when you observe and do what His Word says. This is a vital point for us to make in understanding how abundance and blessing come to us. They don't come to us just because we happen to understand what the Word of God says. *They come when you observe and do everything God commands in that particular area.* Therefore, hearing is equated directly with being a doer of God's Word.

The basic requirement for having blessing and abundance is that we listen very carefully to God's voice. This is a basic requirement for being a child of God. Jesus said, "My sheep hear my voice, and I know them, and they follow me" (John 10:27). How do we hear the voice of Jesus today? We hear the voice of God in His Word. It is the written Word of God that brings the voice of God to us. The key to blessing is hearing and obeying God's voice.

You can read the Bible and still not hear God's voice. You only hear God's voice when you read the Bible and do precisely what the Word of God says to do. The phrase, "...if thou shalt hearken diligently unto the voice of the Lord thy God..."

(Deut. 28:1) means "If you will hear, listening" (Hebrew). In other words, "If you will listen, using both ears."

Many people have learned how to listen to God with one ear and to strongholds of the enemy with the other. They become muddled in their brains and confusion is the result. There is no clarity and obedience to what God says. That is why Paul says (in 2 Corinthians 10:5) if we are going to pull down strongholds, we must cast down imaginations and bring every thought into captivity. *We must listen to God's Word with both ears.*

Notice verse 2 of Deuteronomy 28, "And all these blessings shall come on thee, and overtake thee, if thou shalt hearken unto the voice of the Lord thy God."

This passage points out that the blessings actually overtake us. They catch up to us; we cannot run away from them. There is no way to escape those blessings if we are giving heed to the Word of God. I know a lot of believers who are running after blessings. They are doing everything they can to obtain blessings, except the right things. They have not learned how to hearken diligently unto the voice of the Lord their God and to observe and to do all His commandments. This is the key to blessing and abundance. The verses that follow in Deuteronomy 28 reveal that no area of our lives is omitted in terms of blessing, if we will do the Word of God.

How To Be Blessed

It is so simple to be blessed. The blessing flows to you and me as a direct outworking of the energy and power inherent in the Word of God. This is the central theme of this book. Faith comes to you as an automatic working of God's Word. The new birth comes to you as an automatic working of God's Word. Healing comes to you as an automatic working of God's Word. *Abundance and blessing come to you as an automatic working of God's Word.*

Spend some of your devotional time reading through the first thirteen verses of Deuteronomy 28. Believe that fruitfulness is a blessing from God for you. Believe that abundance is a blessing. Protection is your right. God will give you direction. There is victory over the devil. You can have success in every area of life. There will be holiness in your walk with God. You will have honor and favor among the businesspeople in your community. God will pour abundance upon you. You will be a lender and not a borrower. And then notice, the Lord will make you the head, and not the tail. You will be the one who makes decisions. You shall be above, and you shall not be beneath.

Notice again at the end of verse 13, Moses reemphasizes, "...if...thou hearken unto the commandments of the Lord thy God, which I command thee this day, to observe and to do them." The key to all of these blessings is found in your becoming a doer of God's Word. When you do, the blessings are yours automatically.

Notice in the next chapter—Deuteronomy 29:9, "Keep therefore the words of this covenant, and do them, *that ye may prosper in all that ye do*" (italics mine).

You can't say it any simpler than that. *If you want to prosper in everything you do, then keep the words of the covenant.* Prospering in all that you do touches every part of your life. That means there is no room for defeat, no room for frustration, no room for failure. This is a sure-fire recipe for success in your life.

The Curses

Notice Deuteronomy 28:15: "But it shall come to pass, if thou wilt not hearken unto the voice of the

Lord thy God, to observe to do all his commandments and his statutes which I command thee this day; that all these curses shall come upon thee, and overtake thee."

The Word is very clear, if we don't do God's Word, the curses come. The next verses in Deuteronomy 28 are some of the most frightening you could ever read. The list of curses is long. Take time to read it and to find out if you are enduring a curse instead of enjoying a blessing.

Notice specifically verse 29: "And thou shalt grope at noonday, as the blind gropeth in darkness, *and thou shalt not prosper in thy ways...*" (italics mine). It is very important for us to make a point here. **Not prospering is a curse.**

In verse 48 Moses gives the consequences of the curse. He says, "Therefore shalt thou serve thine enemies which the Lord shall send against thee, in hunger, and in thirst, and in nakedness, and in want of all things..."

That sums up every part of the curse: hunger, thirst, nakedness, and want of all things. That, my friend, is absolute poverty. That is precisely what Jesus Christ experienced on the cross when He died for you.

The Divine Exchange

How can we escape from the curses of Deuteronomy 28? The Book of Galatians has the answer! As believers in the New Covenant we have been freed from the curse of the Law. The curse was dealt with by Christ on the cross. Because Christ paid the penalty, we are released from the curse.

When Jesus died on the cross, He was punished for our sins and in turn gave us forgiveness and reconciliation. On the cross He received our sicknesses and pains and gave us healing in return. He received our guilt and sin so that we might have righteousness. He was made a curse so that we might receive the blessing. He was made poverty so that we might receive wealth. He died so that we might live.

This is the divine exchange of the gospel. *Jesus took all the evil that was due us and gave us all the good that was due to Him.* In other words, He was made a curse so that we might have the blessing. Galatians 3:13 is very emphatic in declaring that Christ has redeemed us from the curse of the Law because He was made a curse for us.

Why? So that the blessing of Abraham might come on the Gentiles. There is no question that Jesus hung upon the cross. We have just discussed that the elements of the curse were *hunger, thirst, nakedness,* and *want of all things* (see Deut. 28:48). Jesus experienced all of these on the cross. He was truly made a curse for us. Because this is a fact, we are entitled to the blessing of Abraham. Jesus bore the penalty of the curse so that we might have the blessing. What a tremendous spiritual truth this is.

The Blessing of Abraham

In Galatians 3:14 Paul says "That the blessing of Abraham might come on the Gentiles through Jesus Christ; that we might receive the promise of the Spirit through faith." What is the blessing of Abraham? Let's look at Genesis 24:1: "And Abraham was old, and well stricken in age: and the Lord had blessed Abraham *in all things*" (italics mine). Abraham was blessed in all things—physically, materially, spiritually.

The administrator of that blessing today is the Holy Spirit. We cannot receive our inheritance, we cannot walk in peace, we cannot walk in healing, in righteousness, in blessing, in wealth, in the fullness of life and in the power of the new man apart from the revelation of the Holy Spirit.

One more point should be made concerning blessing and cursing. *Jesus, on the cross, totally exhausted the poverty curse.* Something has to happen in your spirit concerning this truth; you have to catch its revelation. You have already seen God's revelation concerning your sin. You have seen your sin put upon Christ, and Christ bearing that sin away.

You know He paid the price for your sin on the cross. Now I challenge you to see the same thing in the area of poverty. *You will never walk in the power of abundance and prosperity until you see the poverty curse being borne by Christ on the cross.* This must come to you through the revelation of the Holy Spirit.

You see, again, the Holy Spirit is the administrator of the Godhead. He reveals the blessings that come to us. It is He Who must reveal to you that abundance and prosperity are yours, because Jesus bore the poverty curse on the cross.

Take a moment now and meditate with me concerning Jesus on the cross. See Him exhaust the poverty curse—hunger, thirst, nakedness and want of all things. He was hungry. He hadn't eaten for nearly twenty-four hours. He cried from the cross, "I thirst."

There is no question that He was naked on the cross. The soldiers had stripped Him of all His clothing. They were gambling for His clothes at the foot of the cross. He was in want of all things. He didn't have a tomb. He had nothing to be wrapped in after His death. He died without anything.

Can you see that Jesus was totally in want of all things? Why? Because he was paying the price of poverty. He was totally exhausting the curse *so that the blessing of Abraham might come on the Gentiles*—you and me! the blessing of God's prosperity.

If we choose to live in poverty, we are choosing

to live under the curse. There is no question about this from the text. When you see this simple truth you will catch the key of spiritual revelation in the area of financial abundance. Now you can turn your faith loose. You can be sure there will be no problem with your believing.

Further Evidence

Let's turn to 2 Corinthians 8 and 9 for further corroboration of this truth. These chapters focus particularly on the subject of money. There are thirty-nine verses in the two chapters and all of them deal explicitly with how money is to be handled.

"For ye know the grace of our Lord Jesus Christ, that, though he was rich, yet for your sakes he became poor, that ye through his poverty might be rich" (2 Cor. 8:9).

Paul declares very simply here the same truth that is revealed in Galatians 3. Jesus was made poor for us! *You can't say it more clearly than that.* Why did He become poor? So that we might be rich with His wealth. But notice it comes to us through the grace of our Lord Jesus Christ. And the grace of Jesus is administered to us by the power of the Holy Spirit.

That ought to settle the question for time and eternity. Does God want me to have abundance? Does God want me to prosper? *Absolutely, yes; He does!* In fact, to refuse that abundance and to refuse that prosperity is to refuse the revelation of the cross itself—and what Jesus paid for us on that cross.

If Jesus went through that kind of agony, scorn and shame for me to have abundance then, brother, I want the abundance. Not for the sake of having things, but because that abundance is a part of the provision of Calvary and the price Jesus paid.

Walking in the Blessings of God

If abundance and prosperity are provided for me because of the cross, how can I translate that truth into actuality in my life? How do I apply my faith on a day-by-day basis to walk in the blessings of God? The answer to this question is found in 2 Peter 1:3 and 4 (italics are mine):

> **3 According as his divine power *hath given unto us all things that pertain unto life and godliness,* through the knowledge of him that hath called us to glory and virtue:**
> **4 Whereby are given unto us exceeding great and precious promises: that by these ye might be partakers of the divine nature, having escaped the corruption that is in the world through lust.**

Remember the basic premise of this book is that there is a special, powerful divine energy that flows toward us from the Scriptures, the Word of God. That Word automatically creates faith, the new birth, healing, and now we discover that the Word of God automatically creates abundance and prosperity.

Let us examine this text. "According as his divine power **hath given** unto us **all things** that pertain unto life and godliness..." (2 Pet. 1:3, italics mine). Notice the tense of the verb Paul uses here. It is the perfect tense. It is very emphatic in the Greek language. What Paul is saying is that **God has already given us absolutely everything we are ever going to need for this life and for the life to come.**

Notice he says, "...all things that pertain unto life and godliness..." That includes every particular need you have. The important thing to notice is that God has already given them to you. The work has already been done. Please allow me to emphasize this fact. The work is completed. God has already given us everything that pertains unto life and godliness.

Most of the time when I hear people pray, they are asking God to give them things that He has already given them. Such praying must be an insult to the heavenly Father. This verse tells us that everything you are ever going to need has already been given to you.

One of the great keys of praying in faith is to line your prayer up with what the Word of God says. If God's Word says God has provided abundance for you, then make your prayer say that. You have already received that abundance. But you may say, "I don't see any actuality of it." Let's continue with the text.

The Promises of God

Notice verse 4: "Whereby are given unto us exceeding great and precious promises...." This is the key. God has already given us everything we need now or are ever going to need. And how did He give it to us? *He gave it to us in the exceeding great and precious promises.* Can you see that? Joshua led the children of Israel into *The Promised Land* in the Old Testament. However, in the New Testament Jesus wants to lead us into the *Land of Promises!*

Everything you need is in the Word. It is so important for you to see that. God has already given you everything you need, and His delivery system to you for those things is His promises.

We don't need to ask God to give us more than He has already given. We need merely to avail ourselves of that which God has already provided. The promises of God have everything in them that we need for life and godliness. All that remains for us to do now is *to appropriate and to apply these promises by active personal faith.*

Conditions for Blessings

There are several Biblical conditions revealed in the Word if you want to have abundance. First, your heart must be right in desiring abundance. Get greed out of your heart (1 Tim. 6:10). Then you must not earn your money the wrong way. The Bible speaks against charging unusually high interest rates (Prov. 28:8).

The next principle is don't desire abundance in order to spend it on yourself. We must learn how to be generous and give it away (Prov. 11:24-25). Then the Bible teaches us to bless the poor with our abundance (Prov. 19:17). On the basis of this principle my ministry was instrumental in blessing the victims of Chernobyl in the Soviet Union. God, in return, immediately began to bless my ministry.

Another great principle in abundance is "Give, and it shall be given unto you; good measure, pressed down, and shaken together, and running over, shall men give into your bosom..." (Luke 6:38). If you sow in abundance you will reap in abundance.

Then we must show honor with our finances. First we honor the Lord with our firstfruits (Prov. 3:9-10). We must show honor to our parents so that they are well provided for (Matt. 15:3-7). People who don't honor their parents never have it go well with them. Finally, we show honor by blessing the elders who labor in the Word and doctrine (1 Tim. 5:17, 18).

Receiving the Blessings

By now you may be thinking, "Terry Law, I want to appropriate the promises by faith. Tell me how to do it." Joshua 1:8 says, "This book of the law [the promises] shall not depart out of thy mouth; but thou shalt meditate therein day and night, that thou mayest observe to do according to all that is written therein: for then thou shalt make thy way prosperous, and then thou shalt have good success."

What an incredible promise of spiritual blessing. Notice the key principles of this verse. First of all, you are to think the Word of God, day and night. Meditation is absolutely essential to prosperity and abundance. If you are not meditating in the abundance that God's Word says you have, you will never have it. It must be a part of your thinking day and night.

Secondly, this book of the Law shall not depart out of your mouth. You have to speak that Word all the time. You have to confess the abundance the Word of God says you have. You have to say with your mouth that Christ has redeemed you from the curse of the Law so that the blessings of Abraham may come upon you.

The third condition of this verse is that you do according to all that is written in the Book. We are not called upon just to **think** the Word, or just to **say** the Word, **we are called upon to do the Word.**

Honor God with your firstfruits, honor your parents, honor your spiritual leaders, bless the poor, do the things the Word requires and I guarantee you that the blessings of God will be on your life. You won't have to go after the blessings; they will come after you. They'll catch up to you. They'll jump all over you. Whatever you do will prosper and you will have success.

Let me make one additional important point in this chapter. If you will fulfill these conditions, then the blessings are yours, according to 2 Corinthians 9:8: "And God is able to make all grace abound toward you; that ye, always having all sufficiency in all things, may abound to every good work."

Notice there are two 'abounds' and three 'alls' in this verse. God will make **all** grace abound toward you that you **always, having all** sufficiency in **all** things, may **abound** to **every** good work. I don't know a verse that can promise you anything more than that. Paul uses the repetition to impress us with the power of the thought.

Language can't say more than that. But notice what all that abounding is for—**that ye may abound to every good work.** The key to abundance is to remember you are not the end; you are simply the means to the end. God wants you to have abundance so you can help to finance worldwide revival. God wants you to have abundance so that you can stand behind the missionary program of your church.

I believe we are on the verge of the greatest revival the world has ever seen and there is only one thing holding it back; we don't have the money to do the job. **It takes money to evangelize.** The only way money will be released, is when God's children move into the abundance God has for them.

As you move into that abundance, you must realize that the abundance is not for you. You are to enjoy everything you need and you will have all of your needs met. But God provides over and above. Why? So that His Kingdom will be established on the face of the earth—**so that the nations of the world will hear the story of Jesus Christ.** "...this gospel of the kingdom shall be preached in all the world for a witness unto all nations; and then shall the end come" (Matt. 24:14).

11

Victory Over Satan

The Word of God Works

Oh, how I want to emphasize this truth to you.
The Word of God works. This truth is fundamental
to your growing in God. The Word of God is quick;
that means it is *alive.* It is powerful. It is sharper
than any two-edged sword. "I will never forget thy
precepts: for with them thou hast quickened me" (Ps.
119:93). We are made alive by the power of God's
Word. Every word from God contains in it the power
for its own fulfillment.

In the last several chapters, I have been review-
ing the effects of God's Word. How does God's Word
work? First, it creates faith. Then it creates the new
birth. Healing flows naturally to you from the Word.
Abundance and blessing come as a result of the action of the Word.

In this chapter I want to take us on to two more
aspects of the working of God's Word. First, it gives
victory over Satan. Second, it provides spiritual food.

I. Victory Over Satan

Let us examine the victory of the Word of God
over sin and Satan. David is one of my favorite Old
Testament characters. A quick examination of the
Psalms reveals his tremendous appreciation for God's
Word. In Psalms 119:11 he wrote, "Thy word have

I hid in mine heart, that I might not sin against thee."

There was a special power in God's Word to keep David from sinning. *The Word has a special life and energy that works against sin.* The Apostle Peter says, "Whereby are given unto us exceeding great and precious promises: that by these ye might be partakers of the divine nature, *having escaped the corruption that is in the world through lust*" (2 Pet. 1:4, italics mine).

The Special Power of the Word

The "exceeding great and precious promises" have a special power in them. If we take heed to them we will escape the corruption that is in the world through lust. We will overcome sin. The Word has a special power in it that works against the power of sin.

When David said, "Thy word have I hid in mine heart...," the Hebrew word translated "to hide" means "to store up as a treasure." You can have a lot of things in your heart, but David put the Word of God in a very special place. He treasured it more than anything else so that it would always be immediately available to use against the power of sin and Satan in his life.

David further stated, *"...by the word of thy lips I have kept me from the paths of the destroyer"* (Ps. 17:4, italics mine). In effect, he is saying, "As I take heed to your words, God, they will keep me away from Satan's paths." There is a supernatural direction found in the Word of God that will keep you free from the stain and the taint of sin. There is a natural force in God's Word that works against the power of sin.

As our Living Sound teams have traveled around the world, we've heard a common question from many young people: "Is it right for me to do this? Is it right for me to do that?" I continually point them to 1 Corinthians 10:31: "Whether therefore ye eat, or drink, or whatsoever ye do, do all to the glory of God."

A related passage is found in Colossians 3:17: "And whatsoever ye do in word or deed, do all in the name of the Lord Jesus, giving thanks to God and the Father by him."

There is a tremendous instruction in these two passages of the Scriptures to help you deal with sin. If you are not sure whether something is sinful or not, notice these instructions carefully. First, can you do the thing to the glory of God? Second, can you do the thing in the name of the Lord Jesus, giving thanks to God by Him? If you can, then it is perfectly permissible. If you can't then to you it is sin. That gets to the heart of the matter quickly.

The Sword of the Spirit

Not only does the Word of God provide victory over sin, it also provides victory over Satan himself. Paul says, "...take...the sword of the Spirit, which is the word of God" (Eph 6:17). I love that phrase, "the sword of the Spirit." If the Holy Spirit wants to use a sword, what does He use? He uses the Word.

Every time you put the Word of God on your lips, you are giving the Holy Spirit an opportunity to use His sword. And let me tell you, the Holy Spirit knows how to deal with the devil. As soon as you start using the Word, the anointing of the Spirit is upon you and Satan gives heed to the action and the power of the Word coming out of your mouth. Remember the Word of God is the Spirit's sword. How often we strip the Spirit of His sword by refusing to meditate in God's Word.

Notice in all of the armor of Ephesians 6 there is only one weapon of attack, and that is the Word of God. Unless a believer possesses a thorough knowledge of God's Word, and how to apply it, he has no weapon of attack. *The Spirit has nothing to use against the devil.*

Perhaps the best illustration of the Word of God as a sword is found in the temptations of Jesus in the wilderness. The Scriptures point out in Luke 4:1, 2:

1 And Jesus being full of the Holy Ghost returned from Jordan, and was led by the Spirit into the wilderness,
2 Being forty days tempted of the devil...

Then in the next several verses, Luke outlines thevarious temptations Satan brought to Christ. He told Him to turn stones into bread. He showed Him the kingdoms of the world and said, "If thou therefore wilt worship me, all shall be thine" (verse 7). He suggested that He throw Himself down from the pinnacle of the Temple. In each of the three temptations, Jesus answered Satan with one phrase, "It is written...."

Do you remember when Satan came to Eve in the Garden, how he planted one thought in her mind? That thought led Eve into sin and brought the curse of sin on the entire human race.

Satan put forth three words, "Hath God said?" He questioned the authority of God's Word. He put a doubting thought in Eve's heart. Now, many centuries later, Jesus answers the question of Satan in the Garden: *"Yes, God has said. Satan, it is written." Praise the Lord!*

Jesus used the Word of God directly against the power of the devil. Why? Because Jesus knew there was an authority and power in the Word that Satan had to respond to. Now if Jesus, walking in the power of the Holy Spirit, used the Word of God as a sword against Satan, I don't think I can improve on His method. If it worked for Jesus, it will work for me.

The Power of the Spirit

But notice what the Bible says in Luke 4:14, after the temptations: "And Jesus returned in the power of the Spirit into Galilee: and there went out a fame of him through all the region round about."

This passage of the Scriptures began with the phrase, "...Jesus, being full of the Holy Ghost...was led by the Spirit into the wilderness." The passage ends with the phrase, "...Jesus returned in the power of the Spirit...." There was a difference between the fullness and the power. It was not enough for Jesus to be full of the Spirit; He had to take the Spirit's sword: the Word of God.

When Jesus replied, "It is written," He was giving the Holy Spirit opportunity to use the sword. It is one thing to be full of the Spirit; it is another thing to give the Spirit the opportunity to use His sword which is the Word.

After Jesus used the Spirit's sword against the devil, then He moved in the power of the Spirit. That is the difference between fullness and power. You have to give the Holy Spirit inside of you the opportunity to use His sword. Then you will move in power.

Until you do that, you're just playing spiritual games. Just because you happen to be Spirit-filled, and speak in tongues, does not mean you are going to move in power. The difference between being full of the Spirit, and moving in the power of the Spirit, is the effective use of the Word of God. If you are not using the Word of God, it doesn't matter how much you talk in tongues. You have not given the Spirit the opportunity to use His sword.

Strong Young Men

John says, "...I have written unto you, young men, because ye are strong, and the word of God abideth in you, and ye have overcome the wicked one" (1 John 2:14).

What a tremendous verse this is for young people. How did the young men become strong? They became strong because the Word of God was in them. How did they manifest their strength? They overcame the wicked one.

The connection is very clear. The only way to overcome the wicked one is with the power of God's Word abiding in your heart. It is time we taught our young people the power of God's Word. It is not enough just to memorize Scripture verses; we must use the Word as a sword. The Holy Ghost inside of you is waiting for that Word to rise up against the power of Satan. He's ready to use it if you will allow Him.

The Believer's Authority

The biggest problem with most believers in the use of the Word of God is the authority issue. They are not sure whether Christ has given them the authority to use the Word of God. They are not sure if Satan will respect their authority if they use the Word of God against him. Consequently, most believers never get involved with using the Word. Let's look at this issue carefully.

First of all, has God given you authority over the devil? Jesus answers that question unequivocally in Luke 10:19, "Behold, *I give unto you power* to tread on serpents and scorpions, and over all the power of the enemy: and nothing shall by any means hurt you" (italics mine).

The word "power" is used twice in this verse, but there are two different Greek words for "power" in the text. The first word is *exousia*; the second word is *dunamis. Exousia* speaks of authority. A better translation of this passage would be, *"I have given you authority."* What is authority? Essentially, it is delegated power—power that is given to you to exercise by a greater power.

Let me illustrate. Some years ago, I heard a minister tell the story of something he saw in Mexico City. He told of a group of young Mexican Boy Scouts who were trying to cross the Avenue Reforma in the very heart of Mexico City at the height of the rush hour.

The boys got halfway across the the street and stood on the little traffic island in the middle. Towering over them in the traffic island was a special chair where a traffic officer stood in order to direct traffic. The boys were impressed as they watched the officer raise his right hand with authority and all those big, powerful automobiles would screech to a halt. Those boys recognized very quickly that the chair was a place of authority.

Suddenly, an accident occurred nearby. It created an uproar, and the officer had to leave his chair to go and separate two drivers who were fighting. Of course, pandemonium broke loose at the intersection. One of the boys realized that something had to be done immediately. He climbed on the chair and raised his right hand. Instantly the cars and trucks put on their brakes. The drivers had been trained to recognize the authority represented by the chair.

They knew that the power of the Mexican government was behind the man who occupied that chair. In this case, it was just a small boy. In the natural, that boy had no power to stop those automobiles. Physically, they could have run over him, but they recognized the authority of the chair. They did not want to invoke the anger of the entire government of Mexico.

You may not feel very powerful when you hold up your hand and tell the devil to stop, **but if you**

*recognize that you have been given authority,
then Satan will do what you tell him to do.* Meditate on Luke 10:19 until you know you have it. But
you'd better know you have it. Otherwise, he will
stomp all over you.

Do you remember in Acts 19, when seven sons of
Sceva came to a man oppressed by an evil spirit?
They spoke to the spirits and said, "We adjure you
by Jesus whom Paul preacheth" (verse 13).

The evil spirit answered and said, "Jesus I know,
and Paul I know; but who are ye?" (verse 15). And
the oppressed man jumped on them, overcame them,
and they fled out of the house, naked and wounded.
They were trying to exercise an authority they did
not understand. *That doesn't mean you should shy
away from that authority. If God has given it to
you, then why not use it?* But you may ask the
question, "How do I know God has given it to me?"

Do Something About The Devil

In the New Testament epistles the believer is
never told to pray to God about the devil. It does you
no good to ask God to do something about Satan.
*God has done everything about Satan that He is
ever going to do.*

The instructions come directly to you personally.
James 4:7 is an excellent example of this: "Submit
yourselves therefore to God. Resist the devil, and he
will flee from you." This verse does not declare that
the devil will flee from Jesus or from God, the Father;
rather, it says he will flee from *you.*

The word "flee" means to *"to run from, as in
terror."* Now that indicates authority, doesn't it?
Satan's not going to run from you unless he knows
that God has delegated authority to you. Satan knows
that God has done it, but he's trying to hide that fact
from you. He's been walking over Christians for so
many years and keeping them in bondage because

they don't know that God has given them that kind of authority.

1 Peter 5:8 exhorts us to, "Be sober, be vigilant; because your adversary the devil, as a roaring lion, walketh about, seeking whom he may devour."

The passage continues, *"Whom resist..."* (1 Pet. 5:9). That says it as simply as it can be said. The devil sounds like a roaring lion. It doesn't say he *is* a roaring lion; it simply says he *sounds like one.* What do you do? You resist him. Don't pray to God about him. You get the job done yourself. *You use your authority. God's not going to do anything about it.* He has delegated authority to you and He is telling you to do something about Satan.

Stand Firm

"Well," you say, "what do I do about him?" Use the Word of God. Take out your sword. Declare to the devil, "It is written...." Satan has been doing everything in his power to keep you from coming to this knowledge. Even as you read these words, the Spirit of God rises up inside of you. He tells you to use the Word now. But Satan is trying to steal that Word from you. He'll bring tests against you. He will attack in every way, because he knows that once you see the principle of authority, *his days are over.*

That's why it's so important for you to meditate in this truth continually. You don't get it the first time you read through this chapter; you've got to come back to it and meditate on it over and over again. I've seen a lot of people who have been taught this truth. They've endeavored to act upon the Word of God, but Satan came at them with a frontal attack. They weren't prepared for that kind of warfare. Consequently, they got beaten badly, not because they didn't have the authority. *They had the authority, but they didn't have the spiritual revelation of it inside.*

When the Holy Ghost shows you your authority and you say to Satan, "It is written," then he has no choice, he does precisely what you tell him to do. Glory to God!

Satan is an Unarmed Foe

There is a spiritual principle I must share with you at this point. It is found in two Scripture passsages. First, Matthew 12:28, 29:

28 But if I cast out devils by the Spirit of God, then the kingdom of God is come unto you.
29 Or else how can one enter into a strong man's house, and spoil his goods, except he first bind the strong man? and then he will spoil his house.

Now look at the second parallel passage in Luke 11:20-22:

20 But if I (Jesus speaking) with the finger of God cast out devils, no doubt the kingdom of God is come upon you.
21 When a strong man armed keepeth his palace, his goods are at peace:
22 But when a stronger than he shall come upon him, and overcome him, he taketh from him all his armour wherein he trusted, and divideth his spoils.

There are two different ways to look at these Scriptural passages. First, there is no question in my mind that they deal with Jesus and the devil. Satan was the armed strong man who kept his palace. He had everything the way he wanted. No one could resist him. The world was under his control. But Jesus, the one stronger than Satan, came upon him, defeated him, and took from him all his armor.

Notice Colossians 2:15: "And having spoiled principalities and powers, he made a shew of them openly, triumphing over them in it."

This verse makes one fact powerfully clear. Satan is an unarmed foe. We have the armor; he has none. He's been stripped of his power. Jesus turns to the church—to you and me—and says "There's his palace; go and help yourselves."

There is a second aspect to the verses that deal directly with you. Because Christ has defeated Satan, it is now our responsibility to administer the victory of Jesus. We have to enforce the authority Jesus paid for. Therefore, we have to bind the strong man ourselves. Jesus has obviously done it; we must continue to do it.

That's what Matthew means. "...how can one enter into a strong man's house, and spoil his goods, except he first bind the strong man?" (Matt. 12:29). A lot of people are trying to take the devil's goods away, but they haven't learned how to bind him. Most of their spiritual strength is spent in trying to ward off his attacks because they haven't learned how to bind the strong man.

When you see the authority principle and realize God has delegated that authority to you, then you will bind the strong man. You might ask, "Who is the strong man?"

Identifying the Strong Man

Paul says, "For we wrestle not against flesh and blood, but against principalities, against powers, against the rulers of the darkness of this world, against spiritual wickedness in high places" (Eph. 6:12). He outlines four different kinds of strong men—princes, powers, rulers, and wicked spirituals. In 2 Corinthians 10:4 Paul calls them strongholds. He says our weapons are mighty to pull down strongholds.

Daniel names a spiritual prince (see Daniel 10), who is called the Prince of the kingdom of Persia. At the end of the chapter, he names a prince of the kingdom of Grecia. There are evil spiritual princes ruling over nations, cities, states, and communities, and it is our business to pull them down.

I have come to recognize this in my overseas ministry. When I enter certain countries, I am able to identify the stronghold that rules in that country. I face a certain kind of strong man in the Soviet Union. I face another kind of strong man in Poland. I have learned how to identify them spiritually.

I will never forget something that happened in the month of May, 1981. I was in a charismatic leadership conference in St. Louis where many men of God from around America and other parts of the world were gathered together. Most of the historic denominations were represented. Derek Prince was teaching the group on spiritual warfare.

My office called from Tulsa with a message for me. Just a few minutes before, there had been an assassination attempt on Pope John Paul II. I had one of my Living Sound teams in Poland at that very moment, and my office was deeply concerned with the effect of the news on the Polish people. When the message was brought in, Brother Prince addressed the group.

He said, "I perceive there is an evil strong man behind this. Let us go to prayer and see what direction the Holy Spirit gives us." Everyone in the room went to their knees. As soon as I got on my knees, a wave of blackness enveloped my spirit. It was exactly the same sensation I encountered many times in the Soviet Union. I immediately knew the identity of the strong man involved. I stood up and said, "Gentlemen, the strong man behind this assassination attempt comes from the Soviet Union."

As the story began to develop in the press, it turned out that the assassin, from all appearances, was a right-wing, Turkish Muslin fundamentalist. It seemed that he had no connection with Moscow or with the communist world at all. It was only after many months of intensive investigation that Israeli intelligence uncovered a connection between him and the Bulgarian Secret Police.

Further investigation showed that the Soviet KGB had been directly involved in training him to assassinate the Pope. I had no access to that information from the press, but I knew something in the spirit instantly.

God wants His people to move in these dimensions. He has placed the power of binding and loosing in the Church. "Whatever you bind on earth shall be bound in heaven," Jesus said. "Whatever you loose on earth shall be loosed in heaven."

The time has come for the believer to stand in His authority. When you do, you are going to see a mighty manifestation of the power of God. But understand this, your authority is directly related to the Word of God.

If you are going to resist Satan, resist him with the Word. If you are going to rebuke Satan, rebuke him with the Word. If you are going to bind Satan, bind him with the Word. You are God's delegated authority, but it is absolutely necessary, that in utilizing your authority, you utilize God's Word.

God's Word operates with incredible power when you handle it with authority. It is an unbeatable combination. Satan knows the power is in the Word; Satan knows the power is in you. With you and the Word, there is no way he can resist. Glory to God!

II. Spiritual Nourishment

The next effect naturally produced by the Word of God is spiritual nourishment. God's

Word provides spiritual food for every stage of Christian growth. God's Word is so rich and varied that it contains nourishment adapted to every stage of spiritual development. When you experience the new birth, when you are born again, you become a spiritual baby in Christ. It is absolutely essential for you to receive the proper kind of spiritual nourishment to maintain life and to promote growth. God's Word will meet your need at every level.

The Word is Milk

Peter says in 1 Peter 2:1, 2:

> 1 **Wherefore laying aside all malice, and all guile, and hypocrisies, and envies, and all evil speakings,**
> 2 **As newborn babes, desire the sincere milk of the word, that ye may grow thereby.**

These verses indicate that **the Word has milk for babies.** Newborn babies are to desire that milk. If they desire it and drink it, they will grow thereby. That milk is absolutely essential to their health and growth. But notice what Peter says (in verse 1), "Wherefore laying aside all malice, and all guile, and hypocrisies, and envies, and all evil speakings."

If you are going to get full value from the milk of God's Word, you have to get these things out of your life. In other words, they make the milk of God's Word go sour.

We have a little baby in our home; her name is Laurie Ann. there is one thing I've noticed about her that is characteristic of all babies. **She wants to put everything in her mouth.** We have learned that anything that's left on the floor—pennies, screws, pencils, everything—will end up in her mouth. As newborn babes, it's so important to get the right Word of God in your mouth. Stay away from bad things that poison you. Stay away from questionable teachings and doctrines. One of the first things you must do as a newborn babe is to learn how to discriminate among things that go into your mouth.

Another characteristic of babies is that **they cry a lot,** especially when they can't have their bottles. There comes a time, as a baby grows older, when it must be weaned from its bottle. David writes, "Surely I have behaved and quieted myself, as a child that is weaned of his mother: my soul is even as a weaned child" (Ps. 131:2). There comes a time when you have to give up the bottle. The time to start eating solid food has come.

Over the years, I have seen a lot of believers who want to remain spiritual babies. They are constantly insisting that the pastor should "change their diapers." If you drink the sincere milk of the Word, you will grow thereby. You are going to get to a point where you graduate to the next stage. But rest assured, when you reach the next stage, the Word of God will have food for you there as well.

The Word is Bread

In Matthew's gospel we read that when Christ was tempted by Satan (to turn stones into bread) He replied, "...It is written, **Man shall not live by bread alone, but by every word** that proceedeth out of the mouth of God" (Matt. 4:4, italics mine). In this verse Jesus indicates that **God's Word is spiritual bread.** As you know, bread is the main staple item in a man's diet. It is the source of strength. Children love to eat bread. The Word of God has every bit of nourishment necessary for the childhood stage of your spiritual growth.

Shirley and I also have teenagers in our home, and we have learned that **one of the primary things we have to teach them is discipline.** You can tell them what to do, but that doesn't necessarily mean they are going to do it. You have to follow up, to make sure they follow through. A tremendous spiritual discipline comes to us through the bread of God's Word. It teaches us integrity. It teaches us to shun the unreliability and the instability of the world.

Another thing we notice about our teenagers is that **they love to talk.** A typical conversation on the telephone may involve almost everyone in their class. The Bible has a lot to say about our speaking. It instructs us to shun evil speaking. It tells us not to always be talking about ourselves.

"Neither filthiness, nor foolish talking, nor jesting, which are not convenient: but rather giving of thanks" (Eph. 5:4). The bread of God's Word will teach us to shun these things.

Jesus said, "...Man shall not live by bread alone, but by **every** word that proceedeth out of the mouth of God" (Matt. 4:4, italics mine). If you are going to grow up in God, you need to learn to eat **the entire Word of God,** and not just the portions you like the best. All of God's Word is food for you and if you don't eat it **all,** you will lack development in certain areas because of inadequate diet.

You know how teenagers love junk food. Don't be a junk-food addict in the Kingdom of God. Some people spend all their time studying prosperity; others spend all their time studying authority. These are important subjects, but don't allow them to exclude other very important foods.

The Word is Strong Meat

The writer of Hebrews says in Hebrews 5:12-14 (italics are mine):

> **12 For when for the time ye ought to be teachers, ye have need that one teach you again which be the first principles of the oracles of God; and are become such as have need of milk, *and not of strong meat.***
> **13 For every one that useth milk is unskillful in**

the word of righteousness: for he is a babe.
14 *But strong meat belongeth to them that are of*
full age, **even those who by reason of use have**
their senses exercised to discern both good and
evil.

There is a rebuke in these words for all of us. We
must make sure that when we receive the Word of
God that we properly apply it to our lives so that we
become spiritually mature.

Apparently, some of these Hebrew believers continued to insist on the milk instead of strong meat.
Notice that *the strong meat is for those who are of*
full age and maturity. They know how to tell what
is right and wrong.

They also know how to lead a sinner to Christ.
They know the kinds of instructions to give a new
convert. They know how to teach a Bible class in
Sunday school. They know how to educate their children in the power of the Word of God. The time has
come for us to grow up in the Kingdom and to
hunger after the strong meat of God's Word.

12

The Light of God's Word

As I have studied the effects of God's Word, while writing this book, my life has been changed. A new surge of power has come into my ministry. I can't help but get excited about the effects that God's Word produces. Let me recap. The Word produces Faith, the New Birth, Healing, Abundance, Victory over Satan and Spiritual Food. In this chapter we will find that the Word also produces *light, cleansing, a mirror, and judgment.*

I. Light

The next effect of the Word of God is light. Psalms 119:130 says, "The entrance of thy words, giveth light; it giveth understanding unto the simple." Notice the words "light" and "understanding" in this verse. They are directly related to the Word of God as the cause. The Word gives light; the Word gives understanding.

One of the interesting observations I have made in my missionary travels around the world is that *God's Word brings light.* I have been to various parts of Africa. In the countries where the Word of God has been preached and where that Word has come alive in the hearts of the people, the standards of the people have been raised. Their financial situation has improved. Socially, the role of women in their societies has been upgraded. It is obvious that there is a light among the people.

The Underground Church

On the other hand, I can go to other nations of the world, such as the Eastern Bloc nations, and I perceive great darkness there. Education is not the same as spiritual understanding. In the Soviet Union people are very well-educated. They have some of the highest educational standards in the world in their universities, but as you move among the people, you sense great darkness. There are no Bibles there. God is mocked or scorned. The light of God's Word has been dimmed by the power of atheism. I am endeavoring to change that through my ministry.

I have discovered that in Russia there are over one million charismatics in the underground church, and yet less than one percent of those people have access to a Bible. We have made it our task over the last several years to get the Word of God to the underground church. I have an assurance in my heart, that as the Word of God comes to them, it is going to bring light, it's going to bring faith, it's going to bring healing, it's going to bring deliverance, it's going to bring victory over Satan.

Secular education is a good thing, but it can be misused. I know many very well-educated people who have darkness in their souls. They have honed their intellects to a razor-sharp edge, but they are barren on the inside. There is a darkness that hovers over them. There is a searching for the light.

Light comes from one place and one place only: it comes from God's Word. There is a tremendous energy in God's Word that brings light. When you ponder the problems of life, when you are not sure how to handle the pressure that society brings, go to the Word and you will have light. Go to the Word and you will have godly understanding.

Life and Light

In John's gospel we read in John 1:4, 5 (italics mine):

4 In him was life; *and the life was the light of men.*
5 And the light shineth in darkness; and the darkness comprehended it not.

In an earlier chapter, I spoke of the *zoe* life that flows in Jesus of Nazareth; the *zoe* life that flows in the written Scriptures. The above verses tells us that *this zoe life of God is the light of men.*

A man will not have light and understanding until his spirit has come alive with the life of God. It is the life of God in your spirit, continually illuminated by the wisdom and power of God's Word, that brings you into light.

The strange thing is that **the darkness can't comprehend it.** The darkness cannot understand the wisdom of God. That's why the things of God seem to be foolishness to the world. They will never understand us. They don't know why we do the things we do. To them we appear to be ridiculous fanatics, but you see, **the life that's in us is the light.** We have a divine light of God attending our pathway. Remember what David said, "Thy word is a lamp unto my feet, and a light unto my path" (Ps. 119:105).

Friend, learn to spend time with the Word. Learn to allow that light to permeate your being. The more you meditate on God's Word, the more understanding you'll have. Remember Psalms 119:13, "The entrance of thy words giveth light; it giveth understanding unto the simple."

II. Cleansing and Sanctification

The next great effect of God's Word is that of cleansing and sanctification. Ephesians 5:25-27 (italics are mine) tells us that:

25 ...**Christ also loved the church, and gave himself for it;**
26 That he might sanctify and cleanse it with *the washing of water by the word,*
27 That he might present it to himself a glorious church, not having spot, or wrinkle, or any such thing; but that it should be holy and without blemish"

In these verses Paul tells us that Christ is sanctifying and cleansing the Church with the washing of water by the Word. This clearly indicates that there is a cleansing property in the Word of God. The *zoe* life of God that permeates the Word has a cleansing action in the life of believers.

Notice how Paul compares the operation of God's Word to the washing of pure water. Jesus referred to this cleansing action in His ministry. He said to the disciples, *"Now ye are clean through the word which I have spoken unto you"* (John 15:3, italics mine) What does that mean? How does the Word of God cleanse us as believers in Christ? I have always been under the impression that it was the Blood of Jesus that cleansed the sinner. Are there cleansing properties in both the Word and the Blood? These are important questions.

The Blood and The Word

John says, "But if we walk in the light, as he is in the light, we have fellowship one with another, and the blood of Jesus Christ his Son cleanseth us from all sin" (1 John 1:7). It is obvious that John here is speaking of the cleansing power of the Blood of Jesus and that the Blood cleanses us from sin. It literally washes our sins away. But, in Ephesians, Paul tells us that the Body of Christ, the Church—you and me as individual believers—is cleansed by the washing of the water by the Word.

A closer study of the Scriptures will indicate that

there are two great divine cleansing agents. One is the Blood of Christ shed upon the cross; the other is the washing of water by the Word. Both are interdependent. Both work together. One operates in relationship to the other.

John, speaking of Christ, says, "This is he that came by water and blood, even Jesus Christ; not by water only, but by water and blood. And it is the Spirit that beareth witness, because the Spirit is truth" (1 John 5:6). This verse reveals two of the primary ministries of Jesus of Nazareth.

First, He came as a Teacher, and with His Word He cleansed. But He also came as a Savior, and with His Blood He cleansed. Then John tells us that it is the Holy Spirit Who confirms or verifies Christ's work. He backs up the authority of the Word and the merits and power of the Blood.

The Blood cleanses us from sin on the inside. The Word cleanses us from defilement on the outside. The Blood establishes our standing before God; it cleanses us from the sin that separates us from God. The washing of water by the Word is for the contamination that comes to us in our Christian walk.

When you go to work everyday, there is a certain contamination of life that you pick up. You hear someone take the Lord's name in vain, someone else tells a dirty story, and you pick up the contamination that life brings. God's answer for that contamination is the washing of water by the Word.

How Can I Be Clean?

Psalm 119:9 says, "Wherewithal shall a young man cleanse his way? by taking heed thereto according to thy word." When Jesus washed the disciples' feet, He was giving us a spiritual lesson. ***They needed the dust of life removed from their feet.***

In the same way, He says, "...ye are clean through the word which I have spoken unto you" (John 15:1). We can be defiled from the inside with sin and we need the cleansing of the Blood. We can be defiled on the outside and we need the cleansing of the Word of God in our lives on a day-by-day basis. When we understand that God's Word cleanses us, it makes our devotional time spent in the Word much more valuable. Every bit of God's Word has cleansing properties in it, and when you expose yourself to that Word, it will wash you clean.

Paul says that the Church will be cleansed in this way. The same Word that casts out demons and heals the sick also cleanses the saints. You see, sometimes you get weary, you just get tired and you can even experience fatigue in serving the Lord. We need to sit down and wash with the water of the Word. You see, *the water will refresh you.* As you get your feet into God's Word, you will sense the cleansing of the "dust,"—a renewing deep inside.

The Bible says, "...they that wait upon the Lord shall renew their strength..." (Isa. 40:31). The Word of God will rest you, it will relax you, it will refresh you, and it will renew you. That's why we need to say it and shout it, we need to memorize it and meditate upon it. We need to read it and recite it. We need to bask in it and we need to bathe in it. Praise the Lord!

III. The Mirror of Spiritual Revelation

The next great effect of God's Word is that it is a mirror of spiritual revelation. Let us examine James 1:21-25 (italics are mine):

> **21 Wherefore lay apart all *filthiness* and superfluity of *naughtiness*, and receive with *meekness* the engrafted word, which is able to save your souls.**
> **22 But *be ye doers of the word, and not hearers only,* deceiving your own selves.**

23 For if any be a hearer of the word, and not a doer, he is like unto a man beholding his natural face in a *glass:*
24 For he beholdeth himself, and goeth his way, and straightway forgetteth what manner of man he was.
25 But whoso looketh into the perfect law of liberty, and continueth therein, he being not a forgetful hearer, but a doer of the work, this man shall be blessed in his deed.

Earlier in this book, I emphasized the fact that there are two things that hinder you from receiving the powerful working of God's Word. The first is **filthiness**; the second is **naughtiness.** James says if we put them away, and then receive with **meekness** the engrafted Word, it will save our souls. Then he emphasizes the importance of being a doer of the Word, and not a hearer only.

The Mirror

Notice what he says in verse 23. He compares the hearer of the Word to a man beholding his natural face in a glass. The term "glass" is Old English for *"mirror."* James is actually saying that when the hearer looks into the Word of God, he is actually beholding his own face in the mirror. In other words, *the Word of God is a mirror.* It will show him what his face looks like.

When you walk into the bathroom in the morning and look in the mirror, you look at your outward appearance, what James calls your natural face. In the mirror of God's Word, however, you see other things. It doesn't reveal your outward physical features, but it reveals your inward spiritual nature and condition. It actually begins to examine you and open you up to yourself, and you see what you really are on the inside.

If an unbeliever picks up the Word of God and

214 / PRAISE RELEASES FAITH

begins to read it, he will become distinctly uncomfortable in a very short time. Why? He begins to realize that the Bible is reading **him.** He becomes aware of the fact that he is being given a glimpse inside of himself, **because he is looking into the mirror of God's Word.** He will become inwardly dissatisfied and restless. He will soon become aware of a deep need inside that leaves him unsatisfied. Why? Because the mirror is revealing himself to himself. The Bible is a mirror of the inner man.

The next question becomes, therefore, "What will be our reaction to what we see in the mirror?" When you get up in the morning, the first thing you do is to recognize the fact that your hair is uncombed and you pick up the brush and begin to rearrange it. You brush your teeth, you wash your face, you do everything necessary to get ready for the activities of the day.

God's Word has the same effect for the believer. When you begin to study the Word of God, you will instantly recognize that there are certain things lacking in your spiritual life. If you have been losing your temper, the Word of God is going to speak to you about it. You've just had a look in the mirror.

James says we must not be hearers only but we must also be doers of the Word. If the Word of God speaks to you in a certain area, **then your responsibility is to clean that area up.** Apply the Word of God, and cleanse yourself.

Hearers and Not Doers

The problem with many believers, however, is that they have been sitting in church Sunday after Sunday looking in the mirror. They get up from their pews, go home, and forget what they saw in the mirror. **This, my friend, is spiritual suicide.** You are in great spiritual danger if you come to the house of God every Sunday and refuse to respond to the sin you see in your life as it is revealed by the mirror of God's Word.

If people continue to do this long enough, a spiritual veil comes over their eyes. They become hardened to their own sinfulness. They will not submit themselves to the power of God's Word. Consequently, they lose out on the many great blessings God has for them in the Scriptures.

That, of course, is the negative action of the mirror of God's Word. There is a positive action to the mirror of God's Word as well. When you go to God's Word, don't look only for the sin and the negative. *Determine to look into the mirror and see the positive as well.*

The Positive Mirror

In looking in the mirror of the Word, it's important to see that you have sinned and made mistakes, but it's also vitally important to recognize that through Christ your sin has been forgiven. You have been reconciled unto God. You have peace with God through our Lord Jesus Christ. Have you ever looked at that peace in the mirror and realized that you have it? That's the way you look at God. That's what God sees when He looks at you; He sees peace.

Romans 5:1 says, "Therefore being justified by faith, we have peace with God...." You have it; look in the mirror and recognize it.

The Bible also tells us that we have healing from sickness and disease. At this very moment, you may be sick in your body, but take a look in the mirror. You were healed two thousand years ago on the cross. That is the image God wants you to see in the Scriptural mirror.

Satan may be hounding you today with guilt, telling you that you have blown it again, that there's no way you'll ever be pleasing to God. *Look in the mir-*

ror, and according to 2 Corinthians 5:21, declare that God made Christ to be sin for you Who knew no sin, that you might be made the righteousness of God in Him. Declare your righteousness. Look in the mirror, and declare what God has made you.

Continue to Look in the Mirror

James says, "...whoso looketh into the perfect law of liberty, and continueth therein, he being not a forgetful hearer, but a doer of the work, this man shall be blessed in his deed" (James 1:25). When you look in the mirror and declare yourself to be the righteousness of God, you are going to be blessed; you are going to walk in the power of righteousness. But you have to continue to look in the mirror.

When you look in the mirror, you are going to find out that Christ was made a curse so that you might receive the blessing. God's plan for you is blessing and abundance; look in the mirror. Oh, my friend, it's so important to look in the mirror. Don't go to the Word of God just to find the sin. Go to the Word of God to find the blessing, the righteousness, the healing, the peace. Praise the Lord!

Paul says, "But we all, with open face *beholding as in a glass* the glory of the Lord, *are changed into the same image* from glory to glory, even as by the Spirit of the Lord" (2 Cor. 3:18, italics mine). What a powerful lesson Paul is giving us here. In effect, Paul is saying, "Listen, believer, if you continually look into the mirror of God's Word, if you continue to meditate on the glorious things God has done for you [Paul calls it here "the glory of the Lord"] **you are going to be changed into the very image of what you are looking at.**"

If you are looking at your righteousness, you are going to walk in the power of righteousness. If you are looking at your healing, you are going to walk in the power of your healing. If you are looking at your blessing and abundance, you are going to walk in the power of blessing and abundance.

The principle is very simple; you are changed into the image of what you look at. If all you are looking at is your sin, then that's what you are changed into. If what you are looking at is the blessings of God, then that's what you are changed into. Paul emphasizes this again in 2 Corinthians 4:17, 18 (italics are mine):

> **17 For our light affliction, which is but for a moment, worketh for us a far more exceeding and eternal weight of glory;**
> **18 *While we look* not at the things which are seen, but *at the things which are not seen:* for the things which are seen are temporal; but the things which are not seen are eternal.**

Paul says, "Don't look at the things which are seen but at the things which are not seen." Look into the mirror of God and see those things God has done in you, those eternal qualities provided for you by Christ on the cross. If we keep our eyes focused on those eternal things, the afflictions of daily life will fall by the wayside. They will seem like nothing. The energy of God's Word will become His power in your life. Praise the Lord!

IV. The Word Is Our Judge

The last great effect of God's Word in our lives is the Word is our judge. The writer of Hebrews says, "For the word of God is quick [alive], and powerful, and sharper than any twoedged sword, piercing even to the dividing asunder of soul and spirit, and of the joints and marrow, and is a ***discerner*** of the thoughts and intents of the heart" (Heb. 4:12, italics mine).

The word "discerner" in Greek is ***"kritikos."*** It is the root word of the English word "critic" or "judge." *The Word of God is a judge of the* *thoughts and the intents of the heart.* If our thoughts are not brought under the Lordship of the Word of God, we get in trouble very quickly.

Paul says, "Casting down imaginations, and every high thing that exalteth itself against the knowledge of God, and bringing into captivity every thought to the obedience of Christ" (2 Cor. 10:5). We must bring our thoughts into subjection to the judging of the powerful thoughts of God in His Word.

God is Judge

It is interesting to notice in the Old Testament that God declares Himself to be the Judge of the universe. The Word of God declares this about the Father. The Scripture says, "...the Lord the Judge be judge this day..." (Judges 11:27). I don't think anyone would ever contest the fact that *God is the Judge.*

However, there is another aspect to the nature of God that we should always keep in mind: "The Lord is not slack concerning his promise, as some men count slackness; but is longsuffering to us-ward, not willing that any should perish, but that all should come to repentance" (2 Pet. 3:9). You see, there is mercy in the character and nature of God. *Judgment and mercy both dwell within Him.*

The mercy of God makes Him reluctant to judge us. He is not willing that any should perish, but that all should come to repentence. However, in His own divine wisdom, according to John 5:22,23:

> **22** ...**the Father judgeth no man, but hath committed all judgment unto the Son:**
> **23 That all men should honour the Son, even as they honour the Father...**

Jesus is Judge

This is an important truth to notice. *The Father has transferred judgment from Him-*

self to the Son. The Father wants all mankind to respect the Son in the same way they respect and show Him honor. Because Jesus contains within Himself the nature of God and the nature of man, he understands how to judge man because He is a man like everyone of us. That makes Him a good judge.

However, it appears that because of the grace and mercy that are in the heart of the Son, He too is unwilling to administer judgment, and He transfers the final authority of judgment from His own person to the Word of God. John 12:47, 48 says:

47 And if any man hear my words, and believe not, I judge him not: for I came not to judge the world, but to save the world.
48 He that rejecteth me, and receiveth not my words, hath one that judgeth him: *the word that I have spoken, the same shall judge him in the last day* (italics mine).

The Word is Judge

In the last day, it will be God's Word that judges us. And the fact of the matter is, that Word has been with us every day. We can look into the Book and judge ourselves now and conform to God's laws and God's instructions, or we can live in sin and have that Word judge us, on that Great Judgment Day before Almighty God.

David said, "Thy word is true from the beginning: and every one of thy righteous judgments endureth for ever" (Ps. 119:160). By committing judgment to the Word, God is dealing with you and me in mercy. He is saying, "Listen, children, you have the Book with you. I will not judge you in some arbitrary, willful, emotional way. Open My Word, see what it says, and you can judge yourselves."

John 5:24 says, "Verily, verily, I say unto you,

He that heareth my word, and believeth on him that sent me, hath everlasting life, and shall not come into condemnation; but is passed from death unto life."

The judgment of God's Word in my life tells me that because I believe in Christ, I am a child of God. That puts a tremendous sense of faith inside of me—a tremendous sense of joy in my salvation—because I believe what God's Word says about me, I am justified, I am righteous, I am a son of God. *Praise the Lord for the judgment of God's Word!*

13

Your Decision

I hope you have enjoyed the contents of this book thus far. The material that you have read can change your life. There is no doubt about that. The Lord has set before you a table of spiritual nourishment. You have seen the tremendous provisions of God's Word. But now you face a question that only you can answer. **What are you going to do about the Word of God?**

What you have read thus far demands a response from you. You are in the process of making a decision of some kind. You may say, "I want to think about this more," and thus postpone the decision. That's what most people do. They say, "Tomorrow." That is a decision in itself.

You Must Decide

I want to urge you to face the fact that a decision is demanded and it is demanded now. Because that decision will change your life I have felt it necessary to close the book with a chapter that discusses your decision-making powers. For many of my readers this may be the most important chapter in the book. Please read these pages carefully.

Many believers have become slaves of circumstance and emotion because they won't make a decision to rise above the things that are trying to ruin their lives. They follow one preacher after another who gets them pumped emotionally, who gets them excited, who gets them at the altar crying. But in the long run there is no concrete change in the way they live. In this chapter, I propose to show you why this is wrong, and how to change it.

The human soul is composed of three parts: the intellect, the emotions, and the will. *The primary function of the human soul is your will.* Everything else in the soul, that is, the intellect and the emotions, revolve around your will.

According to the Scripture the strength of the soul is the will. Your strength is not in your intellect or your emotions, your strength is in your will. Charles Finney, one of the great evangelists of the nineteenth century, preached to change the will of people and because he focused on the will and not the emotions, his converts stood. Their faith in God was not based on an emotional experience, but on a transformation of their will.

Jesus Did the Father's Will

In John 5:30 Jesus said, "...I seek not mine own will, but the will of the Father which hath sent me." An important point should be made here. If you are seeking your own will, then it's almost impossible to seek the will of God as well. When you're seeking your own will, your judgment is much more likely to be incorrect. You will not have a sense of spiritual discernment.

It is so important for us to submit our will to the will of God. In Matthew 26:39 Jesus is in the Garden of Gethsemene. It is the night before His crucifixion. The disciples are sleeping as Jesus goes to pray. Listen to His words, "...O my Father, if it be possible, let this cup pass from me: nevertheless not as I will, but as thou wilt." Jesus continued to honor the agreement He had made with the Father. Even when He realized that this decision was taking Him toward the cross.

In John 4, Jesus was traveling through the city of Samaria with His disciples. They stopped at the Well of Jacob outside the city at midday. The disciples went into the city to find meat. While they were gone, a woman came to the well to draw water. Jesus entered into conversation with her and in the course of the conversation, the disciples came back with meat for Jesus to eat. Jesus told them in John 4:32-34:

> **32 ...I have meat to eat that ye know not of.**
> **33 Therefore said the disciples one to another, Hath any man brought him ought to eat?**
> **34 Jesus saith unto them, *My meat is to do the will of him that sent me, and to finish his work*** (italics are mine).

The word "meat" in this text might be better translated, "food." What Jesus is saying is, "My food is to do the will of Him that sent Me to finish His work." Jesus was making an incredible statement to the disciples. ***He was telling them that doing God's will gave Him actual physical strength.*** By ministering to the woman at the well, God had been ministering to His physical body. ***Setting your will to do God's will gives you a tremendous strength of soul.***

Let me say that to you one more time. Setting your will to do God's will gives you a tremendous strength of soul. If you're a child of emotion, there will be no permanent result. God will always speak to you in the area of your will. God will ask you to make a decision. That is why, in writing this book, I close with a chapter on decision.

God is asking you to make a decision now in the area of your will. You will find that once you get your will in line with God's will, then emotion will follow. But emotion is not to lead us.

Our wills will lead us in the ways of God. It is vitally important to remember that your will is ever before the face of God the Father. The one thing that God looks for in you and me is our desire for His will to be our will. That is why there is such a mighty onslaught of the devil to get your will perverted through your intellect or your emotions. Your dealings with God begin primarily in the area of your will.

We Have Dominion

A daily question for every one of us has to be, *"Am I delighting to do God's Will?* Is my soul finding its strength in my decision to do God's will?" Genesis 1:26 says, "And God said, Let us make man in our image, after our likeness: and let them have dominion...." When God made man, He made him to have dominion. You cannot exercise dominion without the action of your will. You must make decisions in order to exercise dominion.

God never intended for man to be a slave of circumstances or external forces. He never made him to be the slave of demons. *The way out, the way to exercise dominion is to make a decision.* Most believers are beaten and defeated today because they haven't realized the importance of making a decision.

In his evangelistic crusades, Billy Graham emphasizes one simple action. That is, he desires to bring people to a decision. The importance of making a right decision is primary in the believer's life. It is dangerous to equate spirituality with emotionalism. Remember, I said emotions are not primary, but they are essential. I don't believe we should ever be ashamed of our emotions. We should learn not to stifle them. But they must be kept in their place. Emotions should not rule us. The will has to rule and tell the emotions what to do. When you make a decision, you make a choice.

In Latin, the word for "character" is a plural noun. It is a plural of the word used for "habit." In other words, your character is the sum total of your habits and you make habits by repeating certain decisions.

Involvements of Decision

Let me discuss with you for a moment, some of the ramifications of making decisions. You never make an unimportant decision. Even little decisions are important because in making those decisions, you are laying the basis for habits, and the habits are laying the basis for your character.

Every decision that you make has a positive or negative quality to it. It either builds you up or it tears you down. In order to make a decision **you have to choose for yourself.** No one else can choose for you. Others may persuade you, they may inspire you, they may pray for you, but no one can decide but you.

Another involvement of decision is the fact that *choice involves sacrifice.* If you decide to go down one road, then you are making a sacrifice in not going down the other road. Jesus stated the truth so many years ago, "No man can serve two masters." How many believers there are today who have given an intellectual vote for Jesus Christ and yet have not chosen to follow Him with their hearts.

This is absolutely true concerning the Word of God. The charismatic church world today is filled with people who have given an intellectual vote to the Word of God. They have never made a heart decision concerning it. You must decide to make the Word of God work in your life.

Invariably, someone will come along and say, "Must I give up this, must I give up that?" One of the great characters in John Bunyan's book, *Pilgrim's Progress,* was called Mr. Facing Both Ways. So many believers are exactly that way. They are looking in two directions at the same time. A lot of church people have their faces toward heaven, *but are rowing in the other direction.*

A third involvement of decision is the fact that *to delay makes the right decision harder.* That is why it is so important to make a decision before you put this book down. If you don't make a decision now, it becomes harder to make a decision tomorrow. The Bible says, "Now is the accepted time, now is the day of salvation." It is when the Holy Spirit is prompting you and the truth of God is alive in your heart that you should decide. To delay will make your will become weak and impotent.

In fact, *indecision is itself a choice.* So many believers today are passive. They hear a good message, they read a good book and they say to themselves, "I really should do something about that." That becomes their excuse for doing nothing. They postpone the decision for another time. *Every time you do that you weaken your will.* Every time you do that it becomes harder to make the decision the next time around.

The final involvement of making a choice is the fact that *the time for decision is limited.* You will not have always to decide. If a plane were to leave your local airport at noon today, and you could not make up your mind as to whether you should be on that plane, at one minute after noon, when the plane pulls onto the runway, your decision has been made for you. It does you no good to make the decision then, because it is impossible. Time has made the decision for you. That is why I feel this chapter is so important in emphasizing for you the truths of this book.

I am going to ask you to make a decision concerning the will of God in your life. It is a basic decision between being a hearer and a doer.

This decision will guide you for the rest of your days. If you make the right one, you will be blessed of God. If you make the wrong decision, you will build your house on the sand and when the storms come and the floods rise, your life will be a washout.

Before you make the basic decision concerning the Word of God, however, **there are two other decisions that every person has to make.** You have to make those decisions first before you make the decision to become a doer of the Word.

Repentance

The first decision is to repent. Perhaps you are surprised when I tell you that you must repent. Most of us have wrong ideas about what repentance means. In the New Testament the English verb "to repent" is normally used to translate the Greek verb, *"metanoein."* The verb **metanoein** has one clear definite meaning through the entire history of the Greek language. Its basic meaning is always the same. It means *"to change one's mind."* Therefore, the meaning of repentance in the New Testament **is not an emotion but a decision.**

Many people feel they repent because they cry a little bit. But it is possible for a person to feel great emotion and to shed a great number of tears and yet never repent. Judas was like that. The Bible says "Judas repented himself." But the word used there in the Greek is *"metamelein."* That word denotes emotion or remorse and anguish. That is the usual opinion that most people have of repentance. To feel bad about it, to feel remorse about it, is not to repent.

When you repent, you make a decision. *You decide to change your mind.* It literally means to turn around and to go the other way, *to do an about-face.* Essentially repentance is an inner change in your mind resulting in a turnaround that sends you in a completely new direction.

The best example in Scripture is the Prodigal Son. Not until he was in the pigpen, hungry, lonely, with his money gone, did he come to himself. Then he made a decision. In Luke 15:18 he said, "I will arise and go to my father...." Now friend, that is repentance.

You may say, "Terry Law, why are you talking to me about repentance? I have already given my heart to Christ. I am already a believer." I have good reason, and it is this. In the New Testament, true repentance must always go before true faith. You cannot have a great faith built inside of you without true repentance preceding it.

Repentance in the New Testament

Have you noticed in the Gospels when John the Baptist came preaching, he called the nation to repentance. He told them that Jesus would not be revealed to them until they had repented first. In Mark 1:14, 15, the first message that Jesus Himself preached was, "...repent ye, and believe the gospel."

Notice, first Jesus commanded them to repent and then he told them they must believe. Even after His death and resurrection, when Jesus sent the disciples into all the earth to preach the gospel, according to Luke 24:46, 47 we read:

> **46 And [he, Jesus] said unto them, Thus it is written, and thus it behoved Christ to suffer, and to rise from the dead the third day:**
> **47 And that repentance and remission of sins should be preached in his name among all nations, beginning at Jerusalem.**

Here it is again, repentance first and after that remission of sins.

On the Day of Pentecost when Peter preached

that great sermon under the anointing of the Holy Spirit, the crowd was convicted. They cried out saying, "Men and brethren, what shall we do?" Peter answered them very simply, saying, "**Repent and be baptised**, every one of you."

When Paul gave his farewell address to the elders of the church at Ephesus he told them in Acts 20:20, 21:

> **20** ...I kept back nothing that was profitable unto you, but have shewed you, and have taught you publickly, and from house to house,
> **21** Testifying both to the Jews, and also to the Greeks, *repentance toward God, and faith toward our Lord Jesus Christ* (italics mine).

Once again Paul's message was the same—first repentance and then faith. There is a basic message here that every one of us has got to hear. If you want great faith, if this book has shown you that great faith is possible, *in order to have that great faith you must repent.* The gospel speaks to you in every area of your life. *That bad temper that you are dealing with will continue until you decide to repent and change your mind.*

Have You Repented?

We are so used to tolerating things in ourselves that we would never tolerate in someone else. There comes a time when the Word of God searches us and reveals the sin. When you experience that moment then you must repent. So many believers remain in indecision about their anger, about their lust, about their doubt and their fear. So many believers have resentment built up inside of their heart against other people. You can't have great faith until you repent.

You've got to make up your mind that it is finished. You've got to quit tolerating it. You've got to say to yourself, "This is it, no more. I'm getting rid of this. I'm repenting, I'm getting it out of my life."

Most of the vital things in your life are settled by decision, and faith is one of them. One decision can change your life and bring a flood of faith and revelation from the Word of God to you. *But the basic word that you have to hear at this moment is the word "repent."*

Forgiveness

The second decision that you must make in order to move into the good things of God is *forgiveness. One basic thing that you must understand about forgiveness is that forgiveness is a decision and not an emotion.* There does not have to be any emotion in forgiveness at all. In fact, you probably won't feel like it when you make the decision to forgive someone.

This area is one of the primary areas where Satan has robbed the church of its power. Many believers are walking around with unforgiveness in their hearts toward someone who has wronged them. Consequently, they are not in a position to apply the Word of God. They simply cannot be a doer of the Word. This is a primary area of bondage for the people of God.

In the Lord's Prayer Jesus teaches us to pray, "And forgive us our debts, as we forgive our debtors" (Matt. 6:12). Later on at the end of the prayer, Jesus teaches that an attitude of unforgiveness is a reason for unanswered prayer. If we want our prayers answered, if we want to be forgiven by God, we must forgive those who sin against us.

Peter came to Jesus in Matthew 18:21, 22 and said,

21 ...Lord, how oft shall my brother sin against me, and I forgive him? till seven times?
22 Jesus saith unto him, I say not unto thee, Until seven times: but, Until seventy times seven.

In other words, He was telling Peter that he should forgive as many times as he had been offended.

Then Jesus revealed a tremendous principle in the parable of the servant who was forgiven a debt so huge that it would have been impossible for him to repay it. Ten thousand talents would have been approximately ten million dollars. That forgiven servant had a friend who owed him one hundred pence, about twenty dollars. The servant who was forgiven his great debt would not forgive his fellow servant his very small debt. Jesus used this parable to teach us that God has forgiven us our great debt of sin. A debt so huge it is impossible for us ever to repay it.

The message to us is simple, if God has forgiven us the great debt then we must forgive our fellowman the small debt. We are to forgive at the same level that we are forgiven by God. You can't really forgive your fellowman until you realize the magnitude of God's forgiveness for you personally. You need a vision of Calvary and of the price Jesus paid for the forgiveness of your sin. **When you see that, then you will want to reach out to your fellowman in forgiveness.**

Forgiving Those Closest

Most of the time, the people we have to forgive are the people who are closest to us. They are the people who know how to make us the most angry. It may be a father or mother who has offended you, or a husband or wife who has done you wrong. You may feel angry. You may say to me, "I don't feel like forgiving them. How can I forgive them if I don't feel like it?" Again let me emphasize, **forgiveness is not an emotion, forgiveness is a decision.** You have to make up your mind to forgive them and to do it now.

I am amazed at the number of church-going believers who have not forgiven someone close to them.

They have been severely hurt. Their lives have been ruined. Recently, my wife Shirley counseled with a young Christian woman who had been molested by her father. She said, "I have hated him for fifteen years for what he did to me." She felt she had every reason to feel the way she did. *But she had missed the message of this parable.*

Often in counseling people I have asked an offended wife, "Have you forgiven your husband?"

"Well, I pray for him."

"That's not the question, have you forgiven him?"

"Well, I love him."

"That's not the question, have you forgiven him?"

"Well, I know he couldn't help himself."

"Again, have you forgiven him?"

"Well, I don't really know."

It is obvious that the wife has never forgiven because if she had forgiven, she would know. When you forgive, you will know.

When you refuse to forgive, you hold the other person in bondage. Like the man in the parable, you send them to prison for a small debt. You hinder their spiritual contact with God for the rest of their lives. There comes a time when you've got to tear up the IOU. That person may have ruined the last ten years of your life. Make a decision that they will not ruin the next thirty years. To do that, you must forgive. It is very possible to love someone very deeply and still not forgive them.

The people closest to us are the ones who wound us the most. When you make that decision to forgive, then you also make the decision to forget. *You do not allow the thing to arise in your thoughts. You put it out of your mind.* You put it under the Blood and accept the cleansing of the Blood. Then you can pray to God, "Forgive us our debts as we forgive our debtors."

Again, let me say it, forgiveness is not an emotion. It is an act of the will. The spirit of anger, resentment and unforgiveness that has ruled your life, will be broken as soon as you make the decision to forgive. When you set your will to forgive and to pray for those who have offended you, immediately there is an explosion of the grace of God within you.

Then you are in a position to apply the Word of God. But it is absolutely futile for you to come to a book like this and expect to catch the revelation of the Word of God if you have, first of all, not repented or forgiven those who have harmed you.

Here is my point. *If you repent and if you forgive, then you are prepared to apply the Word of God.* You can be a doer of God's Word.

Now we come to the reason for this chapter. I have tried to emphasize for you the importance of your will—the fact that there are vital decisions that you have to make. I have emphasized the fact that first of all you must repent before you believe. You must forgive before God answers your prayers. Now we come to the most important decision of all; the basic question of this book. *Will you be a hearer of the Word only or will you be a doer also?* That is the decision. The decision between hearing and doing.

The Most Important Question

You say, "How can I become a doer of the Word?" First, you make the decision to become a doer of the Word. You can make that decision right now. I pray that you will at this very moment.

Then follow the instruction of the Word itself on how to become a doer of the Word. These instructions are found in Proverbs 4:20-22:

20 My son, attend to my words; incline thine ear unto my sayings.
21 Let them not depart from thine eyes; keep them in the midst of thine heart.
22 For they are life unto those that find them, and health to all their flesh.

Notice the amazing declaration that Solomon makes in verse 22. He declares that the Word of God is health. It acts like a spiritual medicine. It's a medicine guaranteed to cure all diseases. Notice also that Solomon has given us instructions on how to take the medicine. Let us analyze these instructions carefully.

Attend To My Words

The first direction he gives us is to *"attend to my words."* If you were walking down the street on your way to the bank and the bank was closing in five minutes, if a friend of yours were to stop you on the street and want to detain you with small talk, your first reaction would be to inform that friend that you have to get to the bank. In other words, you have to attend to business.

This is what Solomon means when he says, "Attend to my words." In other words, **exclude everything else, push aside the superfluous and give your attention to the Word.** This includes the focus of your mind.

We must dedicate ourselves to the purpose of understanding the Word of God. *Attend to His words*, that requires the decision that I've been speaking about in this chapter. *You must make a decision about the Word of God.* You must allow it to penetrate your being, you must receive it with an openness of heart—not with rebellion, not with an unwillingness to bow before it.

Your attention cannot be divided. We cannot be sitting with a television set on or the radio blaring or with our mind on something else. You make a decision to refuse to meditate on the thoughts that Satan would fire at you and, believe me, the devil will try every trick. The telephone will ring, some business will arise in your mind that needs to be attended to. But Solomon's direction is clear, "...attend to my words."

Do you remember what Jesus told the disciples to do when they were going to pray? He told them to go into the closet and shut the door. To me, that is a very practical instruction as a methodology in attending to the words of God. We must make a concrete decision to shut everything else out and to attend to His words.

Incline Thine Ear

The second direction in these words of Solomon is to *"incline thine ear unto my sayings."* When you incline your body it means you bow. **There is something about bowing that indicates humility.** It is the opposite of someone who is arrogant. It indicates a meekness of spirit, a submission of the inner man to the declaration of the Word. In other words, you are saying, "God, here I am, teach me. I am open to receive."

If you approach the Bible with an argumentative attitude you will find lots to argue about. Our seminaries are filled with people who are arguing about the Word of God. They are trying to make the Word agree with their preconceived doctrines and ideas. They have never learned to incline their ear. They have never bowed before the Lordship of God's Word. They are much more concerned with making His Word buttress their own arguments.

If we don't approach the Word with an open mind and a teachable spirit, we will never become doers of the Word. Jesus told the Pharisees of His day in Matthew 15:6-9:

6 ...ye (have) made the commandment of God of none effect by your tradition.
7 Ye hypocrites, well did Esaias prophesy of you saying,
8 This people draweth nigh unto me with their mouth, and honoureth me with their lips; but their heart is far from me.
9 But in vain they do worship me, teaching for doctrines the commandments of men.

Oftentimes, that is what a denomination does. It teaches its interpretations of the Word. We are not to approach God's Word with doctrinal prejudice. We approach the Word of God with an inclined ear. We bow humbly to hear what the Spirit of God is saying to us.

Paul knew what it was like to be a Pharisee. No one had more religious prejudice than Paul. But when he met Jesus on the road to Damascus, something happened to his heart. From that moment on, Paul became a man with an inclined ear. Paul's words to Jesus should be ours. He said, "What wilt thou have me to do?"

When you open the pages of God's Word, come with an inclined ear. Say, "Lord, what wilt thou have me to do?"

Let Them Not Depart From Thine Eyes

The third direction in taking our spiritual medicine is this: *"Let them not depart from thine eyes."* Solomon is saying we must not let the Word of God depart from our eyes. What does he mean? One of the great struggles in the Christian life is divided attention. The Bible says, "The double-minded man is unstable in all of his ways." It is possible to focus your eyes on God's Word and also focus them on other things at the same time.

You can look at the promises of God with one eye and look at symptoms with the other. You can recognize it is God's will to heal the sick, and at the same time say, "Why didn't so and so get healed?" It is this double-mindedness that moves so many away from a position of faith. They never experience the tremendous working of God's Word because they have their eyes looking in two directions.

I must make a confession at this point. Years ago in my ministry, I realized that it was God's will to heal the sick. I realized it was God's very nature to heal. It was involved in His name, Jehovah Rapha, I am the God that healeth thee. Yet, I was confused by the fact that so many people were not healed. I was moved with sympathy towards those who encountered tremendous physical difficulties in their lives. To this day, I still don't have the answers to many of my doctrinal questions. I still don't understand why some people remain sick.

However, I have had to make a fundamental decision that has affected my faith. Rather than look at those who are not healed, I have decided to look to the Word of God. I have decided to believe that God's Word does heal. I know that statement raises many questions in many minds. But ever since I took that position, *the sick have been getting healed in my meetings.*

I quit dividing my attention. I quit trying to think up theological answers for something that I could not understand. As soon as I directed the eyes of people toward the Word, immediately there was a tremendous manifestation of the supernatural in my ministry.

The instruction here is "Let them not depart

from thine eyes." If we are going to make God's
Word work in our lives, we have to keep both eyes
fixed on God's promises. If we don't, we become double-minded. James 1:6-8 says:

> **6 ...For he that wavereth is like a wave of the sea
> driven with the wind and tossed.
> 7 For let not that man think that he shall receive
> any thing of the Lord.
> 8 A double minded man is unstable in all his
> ways.**

The Secret Things

Deuteronomy 29:29 says, *"**The secret things
belong unto the Lord our God**, but those things
which are revealed belong unto us and to our children for ever, that we may do all the words of this
law."*

There are certain things we will never understand. In fact, when I get to heaven there are several
questions I want to ask the Lord. But this Scripture
declares one thing: *the things that are revealed belong to us. That refers to the promises of God.*
They have been given to us in His Word and they are
for us. They belong to us. *They are our inheritance.*
They are our inalienable right.

The secret things belong to the Lord. I must
leave the explanations for them with God. Perhaps
one day I will know, but right now it's a secret. My
focus, however, has got to be, not on the secret
things, but on the revealed things. If you will quit
asking, "Why did so and so die of cancer?" and start
believing that God can heal you now, the Word will
come alive for you.

Here is a remarkable truth about natural eyesight. We have two different eyes. We have the ability
to focus both eyes and yet our eyes are trained, even
though they look separately, to produce one image in
our brain. Jesus says in Matthew 6:22, "The light of

the body is the eye: if therefore thine eye be single [if you see just one image], thy whole body shall be full of light."

There is a connection in this verse between your body and what your eyes see. If your eyes see one image, if you are not double-minded, if you look at the promises and respond to them in faith and believe that there is life and energy in those promises, *then your whole body shall be full of light. There will be a physical reaction in your body* when your spiritual eyesight is directed and properly focused.

Meditation

Let us come now to the fourth direction of Solomon when he says, *"Keep them in the midst of thine heart."* I believe Solomon is referring here to the process of spiritual meditation. God said to Joshua in Joshua 1:8, "This book of the law shall not depart out of thy mouth; but thou shalt meditate therein day and night, that thou mayest observe to do according to all that is written therein: for then thou shalt make thy way prosperous, and then thou shalt have good success."

We must keep our attention focused on the Word. *We must meditate on it day and night.* In other words, we must keep those words in the midst of our heart.

In Psalm 19:14 David said, "Let the words of my mouth, and the meditation of my heart, be acceptable in thy sight, O Lord, my strength, and my redeemer." In Psalm 1:1-3 David says again:

1 Blessed is the man that walketh not in the counsel of the ungodly, nor standeth in the way of sinners, nor sitteth in the seat of the scornful.
2 But his delight is in the law of the Lord; *and in his law doth he meditate day and night* (italics are mine).
3 And he shall be like a tree planted by the riv-

ers of water, that bringeth forth his fruit in his season; his leaf also shall not wither; and whatsoever he doeth shall prosper.

This is the key to spiritual success. Don't listen to the counsel of the ungodly. Keep the Word of God before your eyes. Don't have two images. Don't give your time to things that conflict with the Word of God. Rather, delight yourself in the Word. Meditate in that Word day and night.

A Cow Chews Its Cud

When I was a boy I spent many of my younger years on the farm. I've always loved farm animals, cows, horses, pigs, and chickens. One thing that always intrigued me about cows was their ability to chew the cud. I would notice that a cow would take a bite of grass and begin to chew on it. She seemed to chew on it forever. Then she would stop chewing and then after a time she would begin to chew again.

I often wondered about that. Several years later in a biology class in high school, I was informed by a teacher that a cow has the ability to chew the grass, to swallow it, and **then bring it up and chew it again.** This explained the childhood mystery to me.

It's interesting to note in this regard, that the word *"ruminate"* in the Hebrew carries this connotation of faithful chewing. When we approach God's Word we meditate on it, we don't just hear it briefly in a Sunday morning service. You don't just pick up a quick promise in the morning on your way to work and give three minutes of your time to thinking about it.

We need to be like that old cow chewing on its cud. We take God's Word, we chew it. We get the spiritual value out of it. But it's not enough to do it just once. We bring it back up, we chew on it again. In that process, we get the full spiritual nourishment out of God's Word.

Now you see why I have written this chapter on decision. When you make the decision to obey Proverbs 4:20-22, you are making the decision to be a doer and not just a hearer of the Word. Let me recapitulate for you.

To be a doer of the Word, you make a decision. You decide, first of all, to attend to the Word of God. Secondly, you decide to incline your ear, to bow humbly before its authority. Thirdly, you make a decision not to let the Word of God depart from your eyes. You focus on the Word and on the Word alone. Number four, you keep those words in the midst of your heart. You meditate on them.

After you have completed this process, **there will be a spiritual explosion of faith in your heart.** Remember the words of Paul in Romans 10:17, "...faith cometh by hearing, and hearing by the word of God." That Word will come alive in you. That Word will bring about all of the ten things that I have discussed in the latter part of this book. The life and energy for them is in the Word. Your diligence to become a doer of that Word has brought the Word to life for you. Now you must make a decision to apply that Word. Apply the Word of God until you get healed.

Get hold of the healing Scriptures and meditate on them until they heal you. Apply the Word to the area of abundance and blessing in your life. Remember, Christ became a curse for you so that the blessing of Abraham might come on you. Don't let the devil take it away. Become a doer of the Word until abundance and blessing catch up to you and overtake you in everything that you do.

Make a decision to go to the Word for spiritual food every day of your life. Let it be milk for the babies, bread for the young people, spiritual meat for the warriors. If you are in the midst of great temptation and are battling Satan, make the Word of God work against him. Find Scriptures in the Word in the area where he is attacking you. Be like Jesus in the wilderness. Use the sword and the devil will run.

Do you see what we are doing here? We are becoming doers of the Word. We are not saying to the pastor, "That was a good sermon, Preacher. Your doctrine was correct." Oh no, we are taking that Word and making it work in our lives in a practical sense. *If I can get you to this point, I will have accomplished the purpose for which this book was written.* I ask you to make this choice with me now. Will you be a hearer of the Word only, or will you be a doer also? The vote is yours. What choice will you make? *If you decide to be a doer then don't stop until the Word works.*

14
Epilogue
Praise Releases Faith

The Key That Unlocks Faith's Door

Powerful faith was imparted to my spirit as I wrote this book under God's anointing. It is always thrilling to experience faith of this magnitude. My excitement grew as I searched the Scriptures and saw what God promised He will do for *you* as you embark on faith's adventure.

How can we contain such an intense, dynamic faith? What is the appropriate response to such a blessing? Is there a key that will open the door to release our faith?

Most certainly there is! In the same way that God uses His Word *to build our faith,* He asks us to praise Him in order *to release our faith.* "The sacrifice of our lips"—our praise to the Lord—is the key that unlocks faith's door, enabling God to move in our behalf.

It is amazing to see what happens when our faith is released through praise. In one praise service, for example, Jim, a Princeton Seminary theological student reported, "As I sat in the meeting I felt I wanted to contain myself, to hold myself back. My Presbyterian tradition militated against my entering into the joyous praise all around me.

"But then something strange happened. I felt as if I would literally explode if I continued to sit still. Almost involuntarily, I lifted my arms and began to join the others in audible praise.

"As I did so, the dam that held back all my pent-up emotions burst open. I wept. I shouted. I jumped. The intense reality of the experience is impossible to describe.

"Suffice it to say that I felt myself being cleansed and purged, conscious only of the presence of God. As I opened my eyes I witnessed two hot, flaming orbs shooting forth from my chest. I am convinced that demonic entities that had always held me back fled from me as I participated in praise.

"A wonderful peace enveloped me and faith rose in my heart. Somehow I knew, from that moment on, that God was real. The study of theology took on new meaning for me after that joyous experience, and my faith became a personal reality. Always before it had been strictly in the realms of theory.

"Praising God threw open the doors of my spirit, and consequently I entered into an entirely new dimension of living. Praise God."

Jin.'s testimony has been repeated countless times as I've seen God move in the lives of others through praise and worship. It is not uncommon to see unbelievers come to know the Lord in the midst of a praise service because we know that *"God inhabits the praises of His people"* (Ps. 22:3, paraphrased).

Praise Is God's Will

"In every thing give thanks: for *this is the will of God in Christ Jesus concerning you"* (1 Thess. 5:18, emphasis mine). We know it is God's will for us to praise Him because He tells us it is. There are not many places in the Scriptures where God clearly states, *"This is my will."* Why is He so emphatic concerning His will for us to praise Him?

Because He loves us! He knows that if we will obey His Word by doing what He tells us, *we will be blessed!* God wants to bless you, and He has provided you with a key to enter into His "land of promises." Jesus said, "...it is your Father's good pleasure *to give you the kingdom"* (Luke 12:32, emphasis mine).

Praise releases our faith to appropriate the Kingdom of God (and His righteousness) in our lives. Matthew shares an important insight into this truth: "But seek ye *first* the kingdom of God, *and his righteousness;* and all these things shall be added unto you" (Matt. 6:33, emphasis mine).

How do we appropriate His Kingdom—His Lordship—in our lives? The Psalmist gives us some clear light on this question in Psalm 100: 3,4 (paraphrased, emphasis mine):

3 Know that the Lord is God. It is he who made us, and we are his; we are his people, the sheep of his pasture.
4 Enter his gates with thanksgiving *and his courts with praise; give thanks to him and praise his name.*

Praise releases faith to appropriate the promises of God's Word. In many ways it is like the process of resuscitation. God breathes faith into us through His living Word. Our response is to exhale the truth through praise. The Word imparts faith. Faith imparts life. Praise releases faith, and the result is *power to become a doer of God's Word.*

"The Word in the lips of faith," a famous teacher wrote, "becomes just like the Word in Jesus' lips." Praise sets you free to express your faith to God. It returns His Word to Him as you appropriate it in your life. The result is strong spiritual authority that causes demons, sickness and all kinds of bondage to flee from God's presence.

Praise Is Victory's Cry

As I conclude the writing of this book, praise to God rises in my spirit. He is showing me how He will use this book in the lives of His children around the world. Even though the book has yet to be published, I can praise God joyfully, in faith, for what I see Him doing for you.

Through the eyes of faith I see the Word bringing healing to thousands. Praise God! I see Him imparting faith to the downtrodden. Praise the Lord! He is binding up the brokenhearted and setting the prisoner free. Glory to God!

"Faith is the victory that overcomes the world," and praise enables us to release our faith to God so that we can experience His victory in every area of our lives.

The more I praise God for what He is doing in your life, the more my faith mounts in excited anticipation of all that will happen when you allow praise to release your faith.

"It has not entered into the heart of man what God has prepared for those who love Him" (1 Cor. 2:9, paraphrased). The victory is yours! Praise the Lord!

About the Author

Terry Law, president and founder of Terry Law Ministries, has become one of America's foremost speakers on Praise and Worship. Focusing on spiritual warfare through the Word of God, he has seen supernatural miracles take place in people's lives as they have come into the presence of God through praise and worship.

In the late 1960's, Terry Law began an international missionary team called Living Sound. With a special emphasis in world missions, he has led Living Sound teams to minister in over forty countries of the world, seeing multiplied thousands of people accept Jesus Christ as Savior.

An unprecedented invitation to appear at a communist youth gathering gave Terry and the team their first entrance behind the Iron Curtain. Since then he has ministered extensively and has preached to crowds of over 100,000 people throughout Russia, Poland, Hungary, Yugoslavia, and other communist nations. Often facing the threat of imprisonment, he has presented the gospel clearly and without compromise.

His work continues through Living Sound Europe, Living Sound Russia, and Living Sound Poland.

Terry and his wife, Shirley, and their six children reside in Tulsa, Oklahoma. Through his world headquarters in Tulsa, he coordinates the multi-faceted outreaches of the ministry and ministers worldwide in the areas of Praise and Worship and missions with a special emphasis on healing.

For a complete list of tapes and books by Terry Law, including the following new releases:

Praise Releases Faith
by Terry Law

and

Yet Will I Praise Him
by Terry and Shirley Law

or to receive the bi-monthly publication, *Praise Report*, write to:

TERRY LAW
P.O. Box 92
Tulsa, Oklahoma 74101

Books by Terry Law
Available From Victory House

The Power Of Praise And Worship

Praise Releases Faith

Your Spiritual Weapons

How To Overcome Guilt

How To Overcome Giants

How To Enter The Presence Of God

Victory House
P.O. Box 700238 ● Tulsa, OK. 74170

THE POWER OF PRAISE AND WORSHIP

Terry Law tells how his life and ministry went from turmoil and grief to victorious, overcoming power through praise and worship. Larry Christenson says, "...he digs deep into Scripture and brings up a treasure store of instruction and encouragement to share with the Body of Christ."

Available At Your Christian Bookstore

YOUR
SPIRITUAL WEAPONS

In this concise booklet Terry Law shares how
the spiritual weapons of Jesus' Name, God's
Word, and the Blood of Jesus have changed
his life and enlarged his ministry worldwide.
He shows how these weapons can be the believer's powerful arcenal to effectively stand
against the attacks of Satan and thereby enter
into the provisions of victorious living.

Available At Your Christian Bookstore

→ 5:30 at your House Donna
tommarow
San Jose Convention Center

THREE
LITTLE BOOKLETS
WITH THREE BIG
MESSAGES

HOW TO OVERCOME GIANTS

Terry shares insights into overcoming personal problems, financial difficulties, and family and marriage problems, through proven concepts exemplified by David when he faced Goliath.

HOW TO COME INTO
THE PRESENCE OF GOD

An illustrated discussion of the Old Testament Tabernacle and related furnishings and how they typify the believer's approach to God under New Testament (new covenant) provisions.

HOW TO OVERCOME GUILT

Shows how Satan cleverly uses guilt to effectively hinder Christians in their spiritual walk. Gives practical, Scriptural insights for dealing with this common problem.

Available At Your Christian Bookstore